TAKEN DOWN IN EVIDENCE

Taken Down in Evidence

IRELAND FROM THE BACK SEAT OF A PATROL CAR

Gill & Macmillan Ltd

Goldenbridge

Dublin 8

with associated companies throughout the world

© Leo Regan 1995

0 7171 2328 6

Design and print origination by Identikit Design Consultants, Dublin

Printed by The Bath Press

A catalogue record is available for this book
from the British Library.

1   3   5   4   2

Acknowledgments

Taken Down In Evidence was supported by the Irish Arts Council
and a Dublin Corporation Arts Scholarship.

Thanks to the following for their help and support:
Donna Benson, Brendan Bourke, Bill Buford and *Granta* magazine,
Michael Collins and the *Daily Telegraph* magazine,
Gallery of Photography (Dublin),
Katz Pictures, Francis Hodgson,
Heino Juhanson, Gerard Maguire, Shane McCarthy and
Kip Carroll at Lad Lane Studios, Bill McCormick,
Mick and Joan O'Regan, Sean O'Regan, Louise O'Regan,
The Photographers Gallery & Bookshop (London),
Fergal Tobin, Donovan Wylie and, most importantly,
all members of An Garda Síochána.

As a courtesy the names of the individuals interviewed in
Taken Down in Evidence have been changed.

Introduction

We were travelling fast the wrong way down a one-way street. A voice was screaming from the police radio, 'Ram the bastards, ram the bastards!' Our driver swerved the patrol car into the joyriders' path. They in turn ploughed into our wing, forcing us to one side, and kept going. We caught up again and careered into them, but they wouldn't give up. Both cars, now mangled and locked together, were screeching noisily towards the main street. The garda in the passenger seat was leaning out of his window smashing the driver's window with his baton yelling, 'Stop, you little fucker!'

Flashing blue lights appeared from all directions as patrol cars, hearing the commotion on their radios, came to give assistance and quickly began blocking every possible escape route. The joyriders had nowhere to go. But they tried anyway. The stolen car made a final reckless lunge in a useless attempt to squeeze through the blockade of garda vehicles and the chase came to a grinding halt.

Everybody jumped out bar the three distraught teenagers who were held captive between two patrol cars. Gardaí descended on the wreckage. I was barely on my feet when an enormous garda grabbed hold of my camera bellowing, 'No photographs!' Behind him a plain-clothes detective was running towards me with his baton held high in the head-breaking position. I desperately scanned the throng for a familiar face in a uniform. 'He's alright,' I heard my driver call out, to my great relief, 'He's with us.' Behind him I could see the last joyrider being hauled through the shattered windscreen. That was the photograph I wanted. But it was too late. In seconds it was all over. Joyriders bundled into the back of a van, gone.

I was warned about this.

Many people see the police as a secretive, insular lot. I did. And in many ways they are. The police have a unique and powerful position in society. Every day they deal with a vast, complex range of human behaviour and predicaments.

I wanted to document Ireland from their perspective. I asked for and was granted permission to travel across the country and photograph the gardaí at work. I am not, as I know many gardaí suspect, related to the commissioner. In fact I have no relatives in the force. I think I just approached them at the right time.

It's true that gardaí are inherently suspicious. The busier the station, the greater the paranoia. And it's not just because they work with liars, thieves, rapists and murderers. There's a general hit-list. They don't trust the media. They feel, although few would admit it, that they routinely put themselves under considerable risk for the benefit of others and the only time they make the news is when they are caught offside, or when a complaint is made against them. Gardaí are hypersensitive and critical reports are taken personally. They don't trust the public either — the public have a tendency to be naive and misinformed. But their biggest grievance is with themselves, the authorities, as they're called. There are accusations of nepotism, preferential treatment, low morale and a lack of support from superiors living in fear of the complaints board and rocking the promotional ladder.

I spent eighteen months observing Ireland from the back seat of a patrol car. I moved between three stations — rural, border and inner city — each one distinct and unlike the other, dealing with a different public and different problems. The attitude towards the gardaí also differs greatly in these areas — from reverential respect to open contempt, from a welcoming cup of tea, to school-children with hardened looks and middle fingers extended.

The hours are gruelling. There are three shifts — early, late and nights as they are called. In a busy station, with overtime and court appearances, shifts start to blend together, days disappear. Days and nights are spent patrolling, driving or walking around in circles, the boredom only occasionally relieved with the adrenaline rush of a car chase or the result of some criminal act. Strange garda-speak begins to creep into your vocabulary. Now you understand why they appear detached and slightly distant. This is a bizarre existence.

The rural rota is different. It's more on and off, with a few pots of tea in between. That's not saying that the rural station doesn't have its fair share of work, but there's a different way of doing things, a different pace, a different temperament. A lot of the time they work when the need arises. In a small rural community people tend to call to the garda's house when they have a problem or a query.

Garda work is predominantly slow, repetitive and often tedious, but there's always that potentially explosive, exciting incident around the next bend.

The police are called when a situation gets ugly and unmanageable. They're not around to see the build-up. There's no time to prepare. The radio gives out the command and in they go, dropped into the centre of chaos armed only with their wits and a piece of wood. Violence, for some, is an everyday thing, a way of life, a way of expressing themselves, and when it erupts we expect the gardaí to get in there and sort it out. The garda has to understand this language of violence and be eloquent in its use. This is what we ask of them.

A detective told me that he felt the public had a sneaking regard for the criminal — a particularly Irish appreciation for the underdog, a romantic notion of someone struggling against the odds, overcoming the limitations of their environment. I know what he means. But I think this sentiment soon fades when you're constantly dealing with an endless line of physically, emotionally and psychologically damaged victims of crime. Years of sorting through this debris of human wreckage must contribute to the moulding of the police psyche.

Gardaí have an attitude, a disposition that can be hard to fathom from the outside. They don't talk openly about their work to outsiders. They're not allowed to talk to the media without permission. I have included some of my conversations with individual gardaí. They would only talk to me if I guaranteed not to reveal their identities. The interviews reflect a cross-section of the thoughts, feelings and opinions that I heard during my time with the gardaí. Some of the interviewees have put themselves and their career at considerable risk to speak openly and sincerely and I am grateful to them for that. I think they want people to know and understand the reality of their job, without embellishment.

I was forever being asked by the gardaí I met, had my opinion of them changed. I guess it has. I grew to like my hosts. Although I never disliked them, I never knew very much about them. I thought they were an elusive lot. I saw the police as a group of uniforms, a collective being, but now I see a group of individuals. I met some outstanding gardaí but I also met a few who I felt would be better suited to another profession. In the end I'm left with a feeling of respect and admiration. Their motivation and ambition, I believe — even if it can become distorted and lost — stems from a genuine desire to serve and protect, to improve our community.

Pages 2 and 3: Student gardaí attend mass during their annual pilgrimage to Knock. Above: The night shift begins in Store Street station. Dublin.

Top left: The public office in Store Street station. Dublin.
Bottom left: Paperwork — filling in the prisoner custody records. Dublin.
Above: Store Street station. Dublin.

Left: The morning shift — a border checkpoint at Hackballs Cross, Co. Louth.
Above: A community garda patrols the notorious Sheriff Street housing estate. Dublin.

Top left: A garda entertains local children while his partner deals with a dispute between neighbours. Galway.

Bottom left: A community garda is shown a marble collection. Dundalk.

Above: A child helps gardaí to locate toxic chemicals taken from a stolen carpet-cleaner's van found smouldering nearby. Dublin.

Overleaf: Fatima Mansions housing estate from the back of a garda patrol van. Dublin.

Hughie O'Leary

UNIFORMED GARDA. 11 YEARS SERVICE.

There are thousands of gougers in this district. You're talking about some little bollox who has no respect for his mother, his father, his neighbours, the police, the courts, business people, nobody except himself. He'll rob. He'll assault. He'll burgle. He'll do anything as long as he thinks he can get away with it. That's a gouger.

Twenty years ago the gouger would run away. Or the gouger would say, 'Sorry guard. I won't do it again.' Now the gouger is saying, 'Fuck you, guard. I don't give a fuck about you. Or your job. Or the courts. Or prison. I don't give a fuck about anybody. I'll do what I want.' They're coming up and they're spitting at the police. They're having a swing at you, 'You're a shite. You're a fucking dirtbird. You're a fucking scumbag.' Just because you're wearing a uniform. There's no respect. The first time you hear it you think, 'What did I do to him? He doesn't know me.' You get used to it though. You have to. If you were to turn around and say, 'I'm offended if somebody calls me a scumbag, a country redneck bastard.' If you take offence at that type of thing then you might as well pack it in.

We have ten-year-olds robbing cars, twelve-year-olds injecting heroin. You could say it's not their fault, they know no better. We wouldn't call a ten-year-old joyrider a gouger. He'd be known as a little shit. A cheeky little bollox. A gouger is somebody that comes along and doesn't just put it up to you, but puts it up to everything. He'll just take what he wants. These fuckers hurt people. They take other people's property. They can enter your life and fuck it up in half an hour. If someone breaks into your house you'll never be the same again. Anyone will tell you that.

In a lot of cases the parents don't give a bollox. You'll find young fellas, five or six years old, running about on the streets with not an ass in their trousers. And the mother and father are in the pub drinking, seven nights a week. Going to the Canaries on their holidays. The young fellas aren't given a penny. They're like mongrel dogs running about. They're not fed. They're not watered. They're not clothed. You feel sorry for some of them. But when they get to a certain age where they know they either take this road or they don't — well, then you have to feel sorry for their victims. You have to.

I think in your first twelve months in a place like the inner city, you hate these bastards. Primarily because you can't catch them. And because you're dealing with the people they affect. You're left to deal with the crying women, the trauma. You think, 'The little bastards did that.' You'd love to beat the shit out of them for doing that to a decent person. Then you cop yourself on and you realise that it's all really beyond your control. And the best you can do is the best you can do. You can't do more than that.

You get into a system and a routine where you see the gougers and you know what they're doing. You know what they've done, but you can't prove it in court. So why put yourself in a position where you're going to hassle them? For whose benefit? The little woman who was robbed last week might think, 'Jesus, thanks guard. You went up and you hit him a smack in the mouth for me.' But then you're out of a job. Your family is gone.

I won't carry a baton. There's hundreds of young recruits and they want their batons. They're walking about in their blue suits mad to defend. In a year or two they'll realise that to defend yourself in the guards is to put your whole career, your mortgage and your family in jeopardy. The best thing to do, it's not a manly thing to do, it's not what the police normally do, but the best thing to do with the system we have is to walk the other way. If you hit some gouger a slap of a baton and he's injured, the job will not back you. The Department of Justice will shoot you out their arsehole like a pellet. Nothing to do with you. And you'll be left by yourself. Unable to afford to defend yourself. There's nobody, even your own rep body won't support you. You're left on your toddler.

I was involved in an incident three or four years ago. I was walking along the street in the evening when someone came up to me and said there were fellas beating the shit out of each other in a laneway. And me being Joe Guard in my blue suit I went round to see what I could do. As I broke up the fight one of the fellas ran off. I held on to the other one. He's apologising saying, 'Sorry guard. Sorry guard.' I could see the first fella fifty yards up the laneway. He picked up a metal sheet about five foot by five foot and he fucked it at two women walking past him. So I says, 'Right.' Let this one off and I'll go after this other fella. I went after him. The two women were petrified. Your man put it up to me. I arrested him and there was a struggle. In fairness, it was fifty-fifty whether I could hold on to him or not. In the meantime, assistance arrived. The observer got out of the car, came up, restrained him, and we cuffed him. The cuffs weren't on properly when we put him in the back of the car. As I was getting into the car, whack, right in the jaw with his boot. Back out. Against the boot of the car. Cuffs. Right arm. Restrain. Into the back of the car again. One either side of him, restraining him. He put his boot through the front two seats and kicked the driver as we were going down to the station.

We got him into the station. Where I work you get all sorts — violent prisoners, drunks and junkies. You're used to it. We put him in, processed him, kept him for a while. He sobered up a bit, we charged him and released him. Going out the door he's shaking hands with me, 'Sorry guard.' Shaking hands with me! Next day in court he didn't turn up. I says, 'There's another one. Another warrant. So be it.'

The next day on the front page of a national paper ... the woman who originally called for my assistance gave her friend, who was a journalist, this story about a 'vicious garda assault'. The newspaper told her they couldn't print it unless she made an official complaint, which she duly did. The story was printed, and everybody made money out of it. I nearly lost my job out of it.

The complaint was that we had battered this civvy in a laneway. And he was screaming for help, he was screaming for mercy. All this type of bullshit. So naturally, with our job being panicky, it didn't go down well. Our jobs were threatened, 'What the fuck do you think you're at? Blah, blah, blah.' No question of, 'What happened, lads?' It was, 'You're a fucking eejit. What do you think you're at? You're going to lose your job over this.' Panic.

The sergeant got a phone call from this individual who was supposed to be the injured party in this vicious garda assault. He rang up and said there's fucking reporters outside his door, and he didn't want to talk to them, at all. 'Can I come in and get the warrant sorted out? Get this over and done with.' The sergeant said, 'Yes.' That was grand.

He told reporters that he had no complaint against the guards. That it was his own fault. That he was acting the bollox, full of drink. And he was sorry and he apologised to the guards. He went to court and he pleaded

guilty and got put into some place to treat his drink problem. The next day
it appeared on page two, in a little column saying that the supposed injured
party had no complaint against the guards. If that fella hadn't said that, my
arse was in a sling.

The Complaints Board is a load of nonsense. They say they've a backlog of
complaints. They're taking complaints of guards allegedly telling somebody
in traffic, 'Get that fucking car out of here.' They're taking complaints
because the guard was not courteous. The guard is getting hockeyed all over
the street at night-time. He's getting bet. He's getting rammed with stolen
cars. They still want you to be some nice fella up the street, who is a decent
skin, above all moral doubt. They want too much out of the one man. A
policeman is only Joe Public in a uniform. That's all he is.

It's a very thin line between doing what is right and doing what is *right*. An
ordinary civvy wouldn't understand. If you come along with an injured party
who's just been stabbed or robbed or had their handbag snatched, the first thing
a lot of them will say is, 'The whip is too good for those bastards.' That's the
general type of thing you get back from an injured party. The guard's view is
just an extended version of that. When he sees it every fucking day and he does
catch somebody offside, he is inclined to go over the top. But having said that,
nowadays, there's very few guards inclined to do that, because guards have
been sacked. And a fella on the dole after being a guard in this country ... very
hard to get a job. No guard is going to put himself and his job on the line to get
a slap at a gouger. The guards who do are foolish. I know of a case recently
where gougers were brought in and they abused female members at the
counter. And for some unknown reason, members took it upon themselves to
feel insulted for these female members, and there was a few whacks given out.
The gouger you're dealing with today has no respect for you or the courts or
anybody else. And if he gets the few slaps, he doesn't respect that either.
He's not going to be beaten into submission. He'll come out tomorrow and
he'll tell stories, and he'll make complaints, and he'll go to court, and he'll
turn everybody else ten times more against the police, whether it's true or not.

Women play a vital role in any police force but it is a limited role. In the area
of domestic violence and sexual crime they play a vital role. After that, I don't

see much purpose for them. Physically, they are not up to it. If I was going into a situation that was aggressive, I'd rather have a recruit two weeks out of Templemore that's a fella, than have a girl that's there ten years.

People will say, 'No, no. Women are not aggressive, they can calm situations down. Fellas won't hit a woman.' The people who are saying those things have not been out on the streets. I have seen women plastered. Racked about the street. Bet. The baton's been taken off them and they've been bet with their own batons. You can't expect a woman, and it's not a definitive thing, you can't expect a woman who's been brought up as a girl or as a woman to turn around and take on a gurrier. It would be unfair.

If you come from the country to Dublin the only people you really get to know are other guards. And if you try and get to know anybody else outside the job, once they hear you're a guard, whoosh! Off they go. There's a thousand different reasons. It could be stories they've heard. They might be a bit offside in something themselves. There's very few people straight down the line. Very few. And those that are, they'd be suspect for something. It's not human nature to be one hundred per cent, all the time.

If you go out — it's happened to me, it's happened to umpteen people — let's say you go to the pub or some social event, maybe the person you're sitting beside was done at Christmas for drunken driving, he has a grievance against the guards. He's not going to say, 'Nice job. Youse are great fellas.' I usually say I'm a civil servant, working for the Revenue Commissioners.

If somebody hears you're in the police, another thing you get is, 'What's it like? What do you do every day?' If there's been some case in the paper, it's, 'What happened there? Was he guilty?' This type of thing. And you're sitting there saying, 'Would you ever fuck off. I don't want to know.' People think that you know all these things. You don't even know what's happening in the district next door.

The guard is a mule, aptly named — a stubborn whore. He's like a donkey, only worse. He'll not give an inch on anything. He'll have his own way all the time. You'll hear it on the unit, 'You're some fucking mule.' It's a lot better than what most people call us.

A mule is set in his ways and if you try and change those ways you'll have stubbornness and defiance. But that again is a compliment.

Because no matter what happens, the mule will always do it the same way. No matter who it is. No matter what the incident is. We'll go along and we'll do it exactly the same way. And if anybody tries to pull a fly one, like, 'I know the Superintendent,' the mule will go, 'Fuck you. I'll do you anyway.'

I'm a classic mule. A civvy would never think of calling a guard a mule. It'd be too abstract. It's much easier to say, 'You're a scumbag, a dirtbird.' But the mules, among themselves, call each other mules. We're all in the same boat together and we'll all do it the way we want to do it. It doesn't matter whether you're the President or the Taoiseach. Ministers have been done for drunken driving and they've said, 'I'm the Minister for this, I'm the Minister for that.' I don't give a shite who you are. But if you pass the old attitude test, you mightn't end up in the back of the squad car at all. The attitude test works right across the country. You're on a checkpoint. You stop somebody with a few jars on them. You tap on the window. They roll down the window and say, 'Good evening garda. How are you? Cold night to be out.' And you say, 'It is. How's things yourself?' And they say, 'Not too bad. Just coming from an ol' party there, so-and-so transferred, it's Christmas, me brother's wife had a child.' 'Ah, you're all right. Head on.' Second scenario. They roll down the window, 'What the fuck are you stopping me for? Who the fuck do you think you are?' 'Come out of the car and sit in the back seat please.' That's basically it.

If you're polite to a policeman, and I'll make a point on this ... the English police have a reputation now that they'll do anybody and everybody. Whether it be the Queen Mother, or whoever, they'll do them. The bread and butter of any police force is the public. Without the public you're not a police force. You're a dictatorship. You have to bring the civvies with you. If you stop someone and say, 'Your indicator isn't working, your headlight is broken, your horn doesn't work, your tax is out ten days, we'll bring you to court, we'll get you fined and we'll get you a conviction.' What's the point in doing that? That fella will go home and he'll be totally opposed to the police and his family will too, and they'll be taught to think the police are a shower of bastards. And rightly so.

Policing is not about strict compliance with the law. The term 'police' means you police. You don't just hold up laws and say, 'You broke this one. You're fucked. You're going to court.' You police. You make common sense decisions affecting ordinary decent people every day. And if you're a bastard of a policeman, you can make life shit for the ordinary civvy. There are enough bastards out there, enough criminals to keep the system going, rather than doing ordinary decent people for something which is basically a financial thing for the State.

When I started out as a very young guard, it was explained to me at the outset, during my very first week, that no matter what it is — a rape, an armed robbery, a pickpocket, a burglary, an assault on yourself, a threat on your family — if you can do him, do him, if you can't, forget about it. That is something I will say about the guards, there is no pressure put on individual guards to bend the rules.

I was involved in a case where I thought I was failing by not getting this fucker done. There was no lies told. It was just the evidence didn't stand up. The injured party was sure but the jury said that because you're sure, it doesn't mean it was him. A very experienced fella came up to me and said, 'Don't worry about it. You did your best.' And that's all we can ask of ourselves.

*Above: A community
garda. Dublin.*

Left: Gardaí question youths. Dublin.
Above: 'Stay away from my tyres!' Children
collect tyres for a Hallowe'en bonfire. Gardaí,
responding to a suspected burglary call, have
no interest in the tyres. Dublin.
Overleaf: An angry mob surrounds a patrol
car holding a joyrider arrested seconds earlier.
A garda (right) tries to calm the crowd angered
by the youth recklessly driving a stolen car
around their estate. Galway.

*Top left: A community garda
tries to quieten a barking dog.
It wisely retreats under the
caravan. Halting site, Galway.
Bottom left: Collecting fines
from travellers. Halting
site, Galway.
Above: A traveller, having
had a few drinks, makes a
suggestive gesture to two
gardaí. Galway.
Overleaf: A group of
drunken travellers are
brought back to the station
following complaints from
local shopkeepers. Dublin.*

Peter Stokes

UNIFORMED GARDA. 18 YEARS SERVICE.

The guard always has a back door somewhere. He'll know somebody. He'll know a fella in an insurance company that investigates claims. He'll know a solicitor. He'll know a priest. He'll know somebody. This thing about ethics and all that ... the guard will be able to nip down there and get all he wants. You'll be told, 'It's not to go outside this office.' All you want to do is hear it.

You don't actually want to know the details of a particular case, but you want to know everything about the fella. The more dirt and rubbish that you can pick up on him the better. It gives you a lever on him afterwards. Like, if you find out a fella has similar larcenies back 20 years ago, it's nice to be able to throw that at him and see what happens.

You could know a solicitor that wouldn't give you an ounce. You might know a doctor that wouldn't give you an ounce. But the guard, being a finely tuned animal, he'd go to the doctor's secretary and get it out of her. He'll find his way somehow. There's no doubt about it. He'll get it. If a guard wants to know something he'll find out. As simple as that. He doesn't mind how he finds out. If you won't tell me, your secretary won't tell me, some other nurse or some other doctor will ... he'll have a contact point somewhere along the line.

It works on favours. He'll break the rules by giving you some bit of information because some day he'll want you to do the same, he'll want the favour back. He might want to know a bit of background on someone. Typical example — last week I wanted to know about a certain crowd here in town who have made claims in different accidents. I rang an investigator in Dublin. He was able to check around and find out, 'Yeah, these boys have claims.' He told me about it. Next week he'll be doing an investigation into an accident down the road. Some fella going around with his neck in a sling. He'll want to know, 'Do you know anything about him? Has he got any previous convictions? What's he like? Is he a chancer?' And I'll tell him everything I know. I'll cut his work in half. He won't have to do half the investigation into him. It works both ways. Everyone needs somebody else. If you're going to go it on your own, you're wasting your time. You won't get there.

If it's in their interest, they'll talk to you. The ordinary fella on the street won't tell you much if there's nothing in it for him. You'll find people talk to you when it's to their advantage. He will come and tell you, 'Johnny is after breaking the window in my house.' If he broke the window next door your man wouldn't see it. The famous 'I don't want to be involved' statement comes out.

You don't hit a person a slap unless they need it. That's the first rule. If you do give him a slap, make sure there are no witnesses. And thirdly, make sure you don't mark him or if you do mark him, make sure there's a reason, like maybe you arrested him in a stolen car and he crashed. And if he does get a few marks, they can be put on the accident.

If they show any aggression towards you, you have to act on it. You can't just stand there and smile at them. You're there to do a job. If you're going to stand there and let this little fecker get away with abusing you and abusing all around you ... he's going to get uppity. Then if you have to interview him you're wasting your time. When you go into an interview room you have to be the boss, let him know that you're asking the questions and he has to give the answers. If he gets one ahead of you and starts getting the upper hand, then you might as well just let him out the front door.

It's different for everyone. Some lads cross the line very quick. Other lads you can just let them talk on. They'll rant and rave, fuck you out of it and all that, but you don't mind that. Fear has them going like that. No problem. He's not going to get any worse. When you put him in a cell, he's going to keep shouting and kicking the door. That doesn't matter. He'll be handy enough to deal with.

It's important not to leave marks. You'll notice whenever we hit anyone, we never hit them with the fist. Always a slap with an open hand. That's what we call a bit of a hiding nowadays. A boot up the back end. Years ago they nearly killed lads in the cells. Before you finished your shift you'd be told, 'Get the mop out, clean the walls and floors down.' There'd be blood all over the place. I can honestly say that in the last ten years I've never seen anyone get a bad hiding.

Nowadays, if you start cutting a fella up, you'd want a good reason for it. I've worked too hard to get this house, I'll be damned if I'm going to let someone sue me in court and take it off me. But you don't think about your house. I think we all sort of think of ourselves as little heroes. We're all glory hunting. You get the smell of a case, you're about to break a case, it's great. It's like being on a drug, I suppose. There's a great lift. You get a great high out of coming good. Any tiny little thing that's going to help you on your way, it's worth it.

It's very seldom, from the point of view of interviewing, that a fella gets a few slaps. It doesn't happen. The only time a fella is going to get a slap or a box is when he's being arrested or dragged in the door. Usually things go nice and handy from there on.

There's nothing as bad as a fella sitting there and two big guards either side of the table shouting at him, repeating the same questions for three or four hours. He gets to the stage where he doesn't know whether he's coming or going. Unless he's a real good one he'll start breaking down and telling you. Just keep asking him questions. Don't give him a chance to think. Keep a fella talking and he'll give you straight answers. The fella that's thinking, he's the one telling lies. That's the theory anyway.

Other prisoners have a habit of talking to you for as long as they can. They keep talking. Keep dodging the issue. They don't go under pressure that quick. They talk about the weather, about football, they'll even start telling you about their friends. But they'll never admit what they did themselves. That's grand, let them rant and rave for a while. If they're talking about their friends, let them gab on. We can go for them the next day. Once they start talking they're inclined to get very gabby and keep talking. What we call the verbal diarrhoea runs out of them. Then you're in business.

You know after ten or fifteen minutes whether you're going to break a fella. You know his attitude, whether he's composed or not. But if you take any provos in you're wasting your time. You're not going to break them. They're trained for this sort of thing. They'll pick a spot on the wall and they'll look at it. And that's it. God Almighty won't change their minds. The only thing you can do with them is talk football. They *might* talk to you about that, if they're in the humour. The ones that you break are the gougers.

There's one fella I know and you just roar at him, shout at him as loud as you can, and the first thing he'll do, he'll crap himself. That's unfortunate 'cos you have to sit in the interview room for the next couple of hours. The smell is evil. Other lads then, they'll start shouting back at you. Once that starts happening you're in trouble. They're getting the upper hand again. You're going to have to stop that.

You go to a house and a sudden death is after taking place. You make sure everything is above board. From natural causes. Then you have to remember that the people there are family. I always found the best thing to do is try to get a priest to come with you, especially a family priest. They're real good at it. Or a close neighbour. If you happen to know the people yourself, it's all the better. You can sit down and have a chat with them, make a cup of tea for them. If you handle it with a little bit of discretion, a little bit of sympathy, you'll have friends for life, it's as simple as that.

I had a case last year — a sudden death. I had to go up to his home and the father took me into the young lad's bedroom. He sat on the bed and he started showing me the way he held the child. This was the second son he was after losing. My heart went out to him, you could see he was hurting. I ended up sitting there with him, I spent about an hour with him. I met him a couple of days later, took a statement off him, he showed me what had happened, the site, that sort of thing. Every time I meet that man he comes over and talks to me. Never knew him up to that. But I have a friend for life now.

You just have to get on with it, whatever it is. Try and deal with it. It's no good going to an accident and getting sick. I've seen it happen. You just get on with it and do what you have to do. If I'm told it's a bad accident I always, on the way to it, say to myself, 'This is bad. There's people dead here. Lying on the road. Imagine the worst.' And if I get there and things are any way better, it's a bonus. And even if they are dead, at least it's not mutilation. So everything after that gets better. That's the way I deal with it.

Some member comes up to you, you done a friend of his, 'Would you square the summons?' Whatever you do, you do. It depends on the summons. It depends on the type of thing. Normally what I do, if it's speeding, I just tell them to take it easy. If it's tax, I tell them to back-tax. With insurance though, I'm wary enough. If I have to pay £500 a year I don't see why some fella should get away with it.

You have guards ringing you from everywhere. I do the same myself. You say, 'How's things in the job? I'm ringing from such and such station. Would you like to do me a favour? You stopped a friend of mine.' 'Ah. Right. Right. Okay.' Some boys do and some boys don't. You can always tell from the phone call. Even if you don't know him. You know what he's going to say. He'd have the bit of crack with you first, and then come out with it.

When you get a summons, there's two parts. A copy is given to the person and the original is kept. When you want to square something, you get hold of the original summons and tear it up. And that's the end of it. It's also known as 'Pal's Act'. He's a pal of mine. It goes on in every police force in the world.

If it's already lodged you have to pull it out on the day. Call a strikeout. You get cute as you go along. You get to know each judge's good points and his bad points. There's one that would be only too delighted if you kept calling strikeout. He'd be only too delighted. His workload is gone. Another judge refuses, 'Never mind with your strikeout guard, get on with the evidence.' What you do with a fella like that is you say, 'Judge, I've no evidence to offer in this case.' That'll do it. He might bawl you out of it, 'What the hell are you doing? Why did you bring it to court?'

Most fellas will square once. But you've no business coming back the next day and saying you got caught again. Drunken driving and dangerous driving, you don't square them. I don't get involved in anything like that. A fella done for drunken driving, the only way he'll get off is on a technicality in court.

I've been eighteen years at it now and I still get the butterflies getting up in court. If you have nerves, you're on edge, you're in full swing. If you don't give a shite one way or the other, that's the day you're going to fall. It's the same with a row. If you're not nervous or afraid going to a row, that's the day you're going to get a clout.

I'd often be scared going into rows. Terrified. There's nothing wrong with that, it's good to be afraid. Keeps you on your toes. The thing is, knowing when to go and when not to go. If there's twenty of them there, keep going. You've no business there. Your first order of the day is to look after yourself. You're not much good to your wife and kids if you're above in the hospital on the slab, or badly broken up. When you feel you can take it on and beat it, then you go in.

When I'm afraid my knees start shaking. I try to disguise it. I'm shuffling around all the time, moving, so my legs don't get to stand steady. Other lads will start pulling their trousers up all the time. One lad on the unit hangs back, he doesn't go in that quick. But he's very good when he does go in. Some are inclined to get thick and start shouting. Everyone has their own little idiosyncrasies.

It's not a cowardly fear. It's not a fear of what's going to happen. It's more of a nervous reaction. A fear of going into the unknown. You don't really know which way it's going to go. The minute you make a move that fear is gone, and the only time you'll get that fear back is afterwards. The other night I was in a bit of a tussle. I sat down afterwards and my hands were shaking. I couldn't hold the biro. The adrenaline pumping through me. Once you start fighting, start pulling lads into the van, it's all gone.

Most fellas, they're level-headed and calm. The last thing you want to do there is fight. You've nothing to prove, and if things go wrong you're the one who's going to court. When you go out your objective is to sort the damn thing out, peacefully if you can. If not, then do the clouting. Make sure you have enough to do it and come out in one piece.

With five guards, I'd go into most places. You'd pick out the fella that's doing all the mouthing, the ring leader. Take the head off him first. He has to go. If you're going to arrest anyone, make sure it's him. And also take the strongest one. Mill him. If you think he's very strong, make sure there's two to take him. Get him out of the way. They'll be looking for a leader at that stage. They get disorganised. You have them where you want them.

There has to be a lot of trust. If a man lets you down you'd try to get rid of him, get him off the unit as quick as you could. If it was a blatant case of cowardice or something like that, he's no good to you. A man can freeze, he can even run away under extreme circumstances. That's forgivable. It can't be helped. These things happen. But a fucker who leaves his partner in the lurch just because he's a bollox, he's no business being there.

There was an incident in this town where a guard got shot and his partner took off running, left him with two gunmen. That chap makes no bones about it to anybody. He will not work down the town at night. He doesn't want to get involved in any tussles whatsoever. He'll tell you straight. He won't do it. Well, okay, fair enough. The man is afraid. He hasn't got what it takes. He should never have been in the job. The fact is he's in it. He's part of the unit. But he's honest. He tells the lads that he's afraid. The boys don't expect anything of him. At least you know where you stand with him. You've no problems with that. The fucker that'll do something stupid, walk you into it, he's dangerous and has to be avoided at all costs.

It takes one good night's graft and you'll sort a fella out, very quick. If he's beside you, and you get a clout from that side, well you know that he's not fucking there any longer. He should be, but he's not. I know exactly what he's made out of. He'd have to be honest. Loyal. And want to be where he is not just because he's put there. And have a bit of cop on, a bit of comradeship. Then you're in business. Honesty plays a big part in it. Honesty and trust. I wouldn't like to see a fella going into a place and raiding it, and then find out the fucker threw away the file on it 'cos he got a few quid. I wouldn't have that around me. I wouldn't like to see lads taking backhanders. I've no objection at Christmas ... I have friends that put a bottle of brandy in the house at Christmas. I don't worry about that. I accept that. And thank them for it. People ring me during the year, 'Can you do this for me? Can you do that for me?' Different things. I do it. I do it because I want to do it. If he feels like he wants to give me a bottle of brandy at the end of the year, that's fair enough. That's grand. But I certainly wouldn't say, 'Look, I'll square that if you give me a bottle.' I've no time for that sort of shite. I think the majority of the lads think the same. There's a couple of them around, but not in our unit. Here, they're very decent, very honest, trustworthy fellas.

They can teach you all they want when you're being trained but it doesn't mean a damn to you when you come out. What really matters is a little bit of cop on. Common sense and a bit of discretion. After a while, it'll all fall into place — if you have the right manner about you. You can talk your way out of things. And if needs be you can give a fella a clout. Clouting, we talk a lot about it but we do very little of it. I suppose we sound an awful lot tougher than we actually are.

*Previous page: Two men are
arrested after attempting to
burgle a shop. Dublin.
Above: A car is stopped and
the driver is asked to
produce his insurance
details at a station of his
choice. He is well known to
gardaí for driving without
insurance, tax or a licence
but they can only summons
him. Dublin.
Right: An aggressive
prisoner is restrained while
being searched in a police
cell. Dublin.*

Right: Gardaí are called to a late-night disturbance in a fast-food restaurant where three youths are threatening the staff. They slept it off in police cells and were released the next morning. Dundalk.

Above: A youth is interviewed about a car theft. He denies any involvement.
He was later charged for a previous burglary. Dundalk.
Top right: A man flees from a lorry holding a hacksaw after attempting to
steal the battery. The garda on the right gave chase and caught him after a
few hundred yards. Dundalk.
Bottom right: A man, arrested for fighting, is brought to the station. Dundalk.

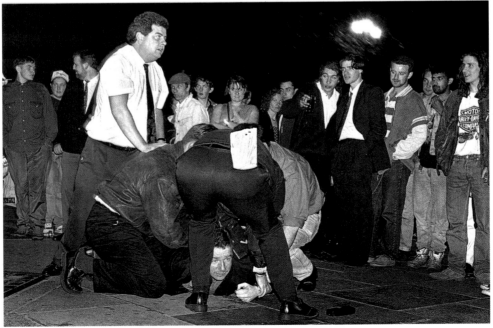

Top left: BOP — breach of the peace — arrest. Dublin.
Bottom left: Late night revellers watch gardaí and a
bouncer as they struggle to break up a brawl outside
a nightclub. Dublin.
Above: A prison cell. Dublin.

*Above: A heroin addict is handcuffed in
bed while his flat is searched for drugs
and stolen goods. Dublin.*
*Top right: Camera-shy youths are
caught breaking into an apartment
block. Dublin.*
*Bottom right: A shoplifter in the
detention room of Store Street
station. Dublin.*
*Overleaf: A prisoner in the detention
room of Store Street station. Dublin.*

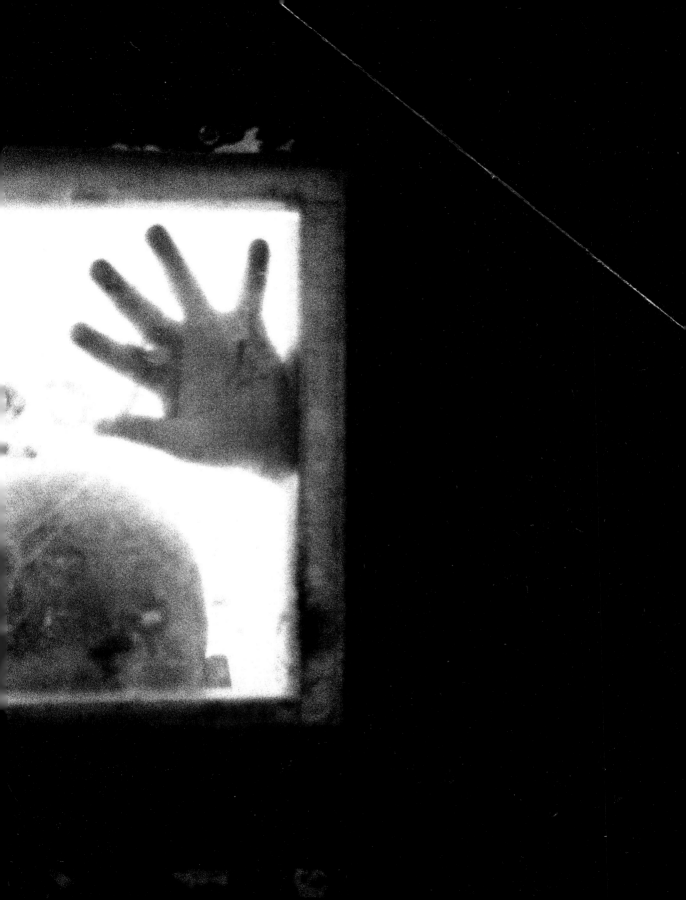

Donna Durkin

DETECTIVE. 9 YEARS SERVICE.

'm more into pickpockets, crimes against tourists, breaking into cars, that kind of thing. I love it. I prefer it to uniform work. I prefer undercover work and surveillance. I get more of a buzz sitting and watching somebody for eight, ten hours, rather than walking around for that length of time and whatever you come across you deal with. A lot of people want to be out, all lights and sirens, chasing cars. If you're like that, surveillance wouldn't suit you.

In this particular unit prisoners are very important. That's what your whole job is based on. Some units you can sit back and do nothing. But you wouldn't last very long here. It's a pressure on you. You'd want to be getting in three, four a week. In a different station it might be three or four a month, and then you'd be doing well. You'd be a great guard. But here, they are there for you. It doesn't take an awful lot to bring in prisoners.

A lot of guards get thick with prisoners. Shouting and slamming books around. But I just go in and talk to them. They think they're going to get a statement by shouting, 'I'm the boss. You'll talk to me when I tell you to.' But, if you sit down and build up a conversation, without even talking about the charge, 'How is so-and-so?' That sort of thing. You can talk to them for a good half-hour. Especially if you know them. If they were aggressive about being arrested, they've calmed down. They know you're all right. They can talk to you.

Most of the people I'm dealing with, they know the story. They know. They come in, they can be detained, make their statement, get a charge sheet and they're off. Most of them are junkies. You see some new faces now and again. When they're caught, they tell everything. They wouldn't put it up to you. They wouldn't go, 'Nothing to say. Nothing to say.' Newcomers — they get such a fright that they've been caught, they tell you everything. They want to get out.

I was assaulted one night, outside the job. It was because I was a guard. He didn't know me as far as I was concerned. He hit me and was giving me abuse, fucking this and fucking that. I think he was mad more than dangerous. I was afraid at the time but when I found out who he was, the fear went out of me. I saw him on the street and he was arrested a couple of days later. It was frowned on because I was a woman. That's what the judge said in court. If I was a fella, there would be no way I'd have been hassled. I was an easy touch. I didn't stand much of a chance. There were two of them and I didn't see a whole lot that I could do.

I'll never forget that one. I was very afraid at the time because that particular fella's family are all mad. They are stone mad. You wouldn't know what they would do. I was paranoid that he would know where I lived. I don't know... I think the mind works overtime.

I told them in work. They were disgusted. I find that where I work the women ... not that they're protected ... I think they wouldn't have been that disgusted if it was a man. I suppose there is a bit of protection there. It's a good thing. There was a warrant got and he was arrested. I wouldn't say we're looked after more. Maybe it's just the male instinct, I don't know. I think that if anything happens on the street and there's a woman involved, an awful lot of fellas would nearly take it personal. As if it happened to them. They'd be all out for it. Maybe a man feels he has to do it. I was quite chuffed there was such an issue made out of what happened to me. It wasn't as if I was bashed up and left for dead. It was nothing like that. I was chuffed that they took it so seriously and did something about it.

I've heard of a driver who refused to take a woman in the car on nights. He felt more confident with a man. He felt that if they had to go to a row, not only would he have to sort out the situation, he would also be worrying about the female. Where is she? Is she okay? It's never happened to me but, yes, it would very much piss me off. He wasn't being sexist. He was saying it in a nice way. He was actually worried. No matter what you think, women are not as strong. A woman is grand, she can stand her ground, as long as the gouger isn't fighting back. It's physically impossible, if you have some mad, drunk, lunatic going mental.

It happened to me one day. There were two prisoners going absolutely mad on the street. I held my ground but I don't know how many kicks I got. The other guard didn't have time to be worrying about me he was under so much pressure himself. A man from one of the shops came out and helped me. It seemed like the car took about five minutes to arrive. It probably took about one. We were under so much pressure. Only for the man coming out of the shop, I wouldn't say I could have held my ground. I find that men think women are not strong but you'd be amazed at how strong you can get when you're under pressure. It's important but I wouldn't say it's the most important thing. There are many men who wouldn't be able to hold their ground either.

I have never experienced a situation where I was totally alone. That doesn't really happen. If it's a violent situation and you call for assistance, you get assistance within a minute. You have cars flying from all over the place. I always felt confident in that ... I called once for urgent assistance and cars came flying, guards came flying. The way I look at it is they're only a couple of seconds away. I'd be confident enough walking around on my own. You know they're there if you need them.

I have heard the stories, on a sexual harassment course ... older guards with twenty to twenty-five years service, they don't want to know. I suppose as far as they are concerned they did fine without women up to now. I've never had that sort of thing said about me. Men complain that they are not sent on these sexual assault courses. But, in practice, they will run a mile and call a woman to deal with it. They think that's all women are good at dealing with. There's absolutely no reason why a man can't deal with it as well. The way it's done — the woman comes in, you look after her, bring her to the sexual assault unit. They do tests, take swabs. But if there is any prisoner to be got, it's back to the male guard. It's very rare that you will get a prisoner out of it. But if there is one, they'll grab him and get the credit for it. That's wrong. They can't have it both ways. They either deal with it or they don't.

I think there is a lot of infidelity in this job but then again, for all I know, it could be the same in every job. But I think it's very prevalent in this job. It might be the hours, the shift work. Male guards have women flocking at their feet. But if I met somebody in a disco and said I was a guard, it would put them off. Maybe it's the power. A man might feel inferior. I don't know what it is. But the men, they attract women. I can't put my finger on it. The oldest, fattest guard ... women will be there for him. Maybe it developed from years ago. When the local guard was God Almighty. If you went out with the local guard, wouldn't you be grand for life. It must have stemmed from that. You see it all the time. You see guards, there'd be women all over them, yapping away.

I'm talking about women who would be in the Garda Club seven nights a week. And their main objective is to marry a guard. They don't care who he is, what he looks like or what he is. I'm going out with a guard and I'm glad I knew him long before. I feel sorry for women who aren't in the job and are married to guards, the way some fellas carry on.

It would affect my opinion of them. These fellas are out at night and they're offside. But if there's some sort of dinner dance or function on, they bring the wives. They're as nice as pie. I just feel that everybody else knows except this poor woman. I'd hate to be in that situation. I would die thinking that everybody knew before me. You'd be paranoid. You'd feel people were laughing at you. Probably these women would never find out. I feel disgusted. I do. I would never say anything. It's none of my business. The only time I'd ever say anything is if one of them was married to a friend of mine. But I just ... no, I wouldn't. Never. It's a macho environment. You have to adapt. When you start out, there might be one or two females on the unit, you feel like you're under pressure. You want to do as well as them. But I'd never interfere. Never.

Constant slagging and comments about women, that's an everyday occurrence. It doesn't bother me. At times, I suppose, you think, would he ever shut up and grow up. But I wouldn't say anything. A lot of them do it to annoy you or to see what you'd say. See your reaction. 'Look at your woman.' If they saw somebody in a doorway they'd say, 'That's a lovely doorway, over there. That's a lovely bus stop.' That sort of thing. It's part of their sense of humour. And it is funny at times. At Templemore, during training, there were three women and twenty men in the class. It was great crack. But whatever it is about women, they just rise to the bait. They answer back, try to defend themselves. It is good crack to a certain extent. But, when it gets offensive, enough is enough.

I wouldn't pay much notice to them. It's very rare that I would. But I have heard of stories ... if a girl was getting very fat, they'd say, 'She must be on the pill.' If somebody said that to me I wouldn't take offence. I'd laugh at them. I don't know if it's fellas in general or just the ones in this job, but that's what they do. The thicker or more annoyed you get the more they'll do it. In Templemore, during our training, I was innocent and young — used to jump all the time. But I learned. If something got bad, if I thought it was a bit much, then I'd just walk off. I wouldn't walk off thick. I wouldn't let them think I was annoyed. There was a comment once, in a disco, to myself and another female guard, 'I'd say she was a virgin but you're not.' Now that annoyed me. But I didn't let on that it did.

I've got used to working with them now. In the beginning there hadn't been a female on the unit in about two years. I felt it was a constant struggle. You felt that they were thinking, 'Jesus. Why didn't they give us another man instead of her.' But there's no problem now. None whatsoever. And that only lasted for a couple of months. When I got in and got to know the criminals, got used to them and the particular job, I was grand.

I won't say you have to be one of the lads, telling dirty jokes, having the crack and going out drinking. There's a happy medium. It's not the sort of job for a lady either. It's not for somebody who couldn't take that sort of slagging, who would be offended no matter what was said. In any city centre station — Dublin, Cork or Limerick — I can't see how a lady would survive. Even with the abuse, the verbal abuse, from the gougers alone. I used to make a conscious effort not to get upset. But sometimes you'd be thinking, 'God, why can't they just let me walk up the road?'

When I was a student I felt sorry for people. I suppose I wasn't experienced enough. I was immature in my thoughts. That's what was said to me. I was told I'd have to toughen up. I think you get hard. I've become a totally different person. Before I wouldn't even ... let me put it this way, I wouldn't be able to talk to you now. I was very quiet. It's a case of having to change. Your mind would be messed up if you were to go home every day and think about so-and-so, and say, 'God love them.' You'd be a wreck. You have to brush it off.

My mother would reckon it was the best thing that happened to me. She thinks that I got great confidence out of it. Even at the training. I am much more confident now. I don't know if that was going to come with age but I think it was the guards. Yes, I do. I came out of myself. The constant slagging in Templemore, it was a good thing. For me anyway.

Right: 'AIDS!' A garda logs a syringe, confiscated from a prisoner, in the custody records. Dublin.

*Left: Picking Lotto
numbers a couple of hours
before the draw. Dublin.
Above: Gardaí respond to
a reported disturbance
but the men have disap-
peared. Dublin.
Overleaf: A garda gets a
lift back to the station at
the end of his shift on foot
patrol. Dublin.*

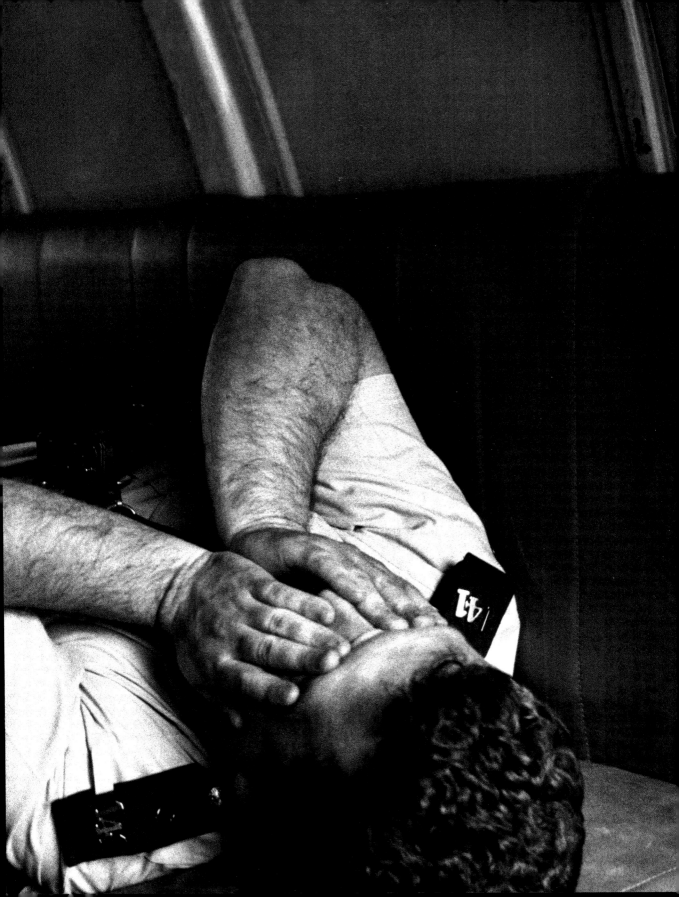

Top left: The station
office. Dundalk.
Bottom left: The communications
room. Dundalk.
Above: A drunken farmer
wanders into the station, late
on a busy night, looking for a
lift home. He got one a few
hours later when things
quietened down. Dundalk.

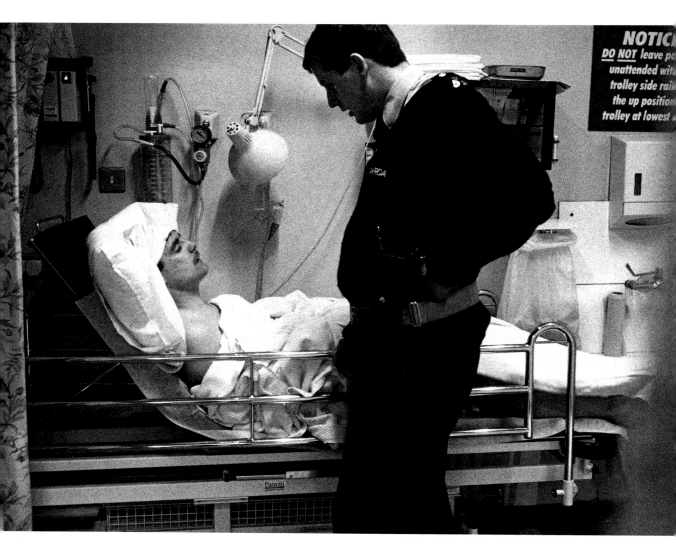

Above: A garda recovers in a hospital emergency room. He came dangerously close to dying in the River Liffey's freezing currents while attempting to rescue a drowning man. He didn't manage to save the victim. Dublin.

Right: Gardaí plead with a man determined to drown himself in the River Liffey. After lowering himself further into the river, he was hauled out and sent to a psychiatric hospital. He later apologised for the trouble he caused. Dublin.

Above: A distraught woman pleads with a detective to rescue her boyfriend who has jumped into the River Liffey after a row. He was later found wandering along the quays. Dublin.

Top right: A post-mortem is carried out on a body. Galway.

Bottom right: A suicide victim floats down the River Liffey. The body was recovered by Dublin Fire Brigade.

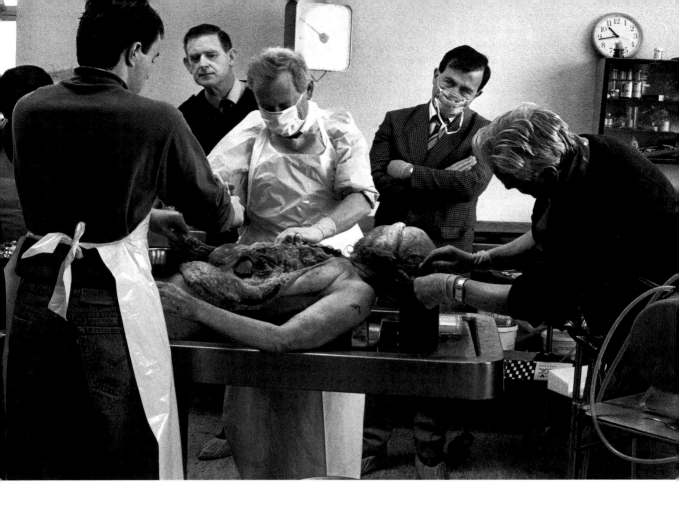

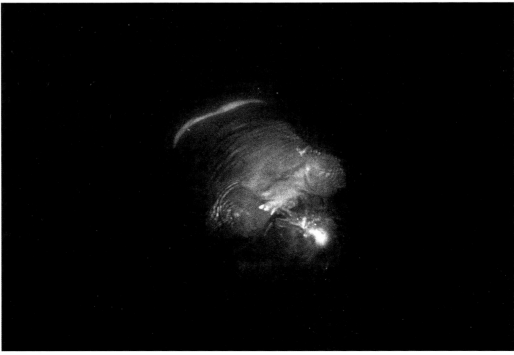

David Meehan

UNIFORMED GARDA. 9 YEARS SERVICE.

My first experience in the guards — I was a Dub — I came into the station and after two months, they knew what my parents did, how much I had in the bank, everything about me. I didn't know the first thing about any of them, with the exception of some of their names. It took me two months to cop on that I was being bled for information. I was even volunteering information in some cases. Maybe it's just the way we carry on.

Most guards are from the country and are curious people. They come from rural backgrounds. They're living in a small town and if somebody does something, everybody knows about it. There's so little going on that you have to know something about it. Gives you this quest for information. You have to know what's going on. Everything is news. News is a way of life. You are dealing with these people and it rubs off on you.

You learn to suss a person out a lot quicker than the ordinary civvy would. You know when a person is being genuine and you know when they're not. If a person is being up front you can see it straightaway. You get to read a person's mind from the way they handle or deal with you. You could add and subtract him on the spot. Everybody. You can spot the bullshitter. The guard will have him nailed in a second. He'll have an opinion of him.

We're inquisitive. We're able to ask questions. You've experienced it yourself. You walked in to the station and nobody opened their mouth. Everybody was sizing you up straightaway. Not consciously but ... have a look at this guy and see how he's operating. I'm not picking you out but your example is the best way to explain it. If you had come in and said, 'Right lads. I want you to stand over here and take a photograph. I want you to do this.' You'd be rubbing fellas up the wrong way. But you stood back.

You were playing the same game as us. You didn't want to upset anybody. You just wanted to blend yourself into the environment, without being noticed. I think that's the trick with the guards. That's the way to get things out of people. To read what's going on. Just sit back, say nothing, and watch.

Everybody listens and watches but I think a guard does it in a different way. It's not like the old lady in the bus trying to listen into someone's conversation. I think we are suspicious, but not suspicious as in, 'Is he a criminal or not?' We're always trying to get as much information about whatever it is, as quickly and efficiently as possible. It's something we do naturally. I don't know how it happens. I wouldn't say we are trained to do it. But that's one thing your existence in the guards will teach you.

I saw a guy on the television last night. Some rock programme. The hair in his eyes. Wearing a pair of shades at three o'clock in the morning, in the studio. Trying to talk as if he's doped out of his mind. He was trying to be radical. He was making up his views as he went along. That guy is nonsense. That's not the way he behaves in reality. He might do it all the time and spend his day doing that. But the inside of him isn't like that. Otherwise he is very fucked up. He wasn't answering the questions he was asked. He had strange gestures, sat with his feet up on the table. So what if that's the way he sits. It was all to make a statement. To convey some sort of an image of himself. It wasn't the real him that he was conveying. He was trying to market himself. He was trying to say, 'I'm weird. That's the way I make my money. If I wasn't a rock star I wouldn't be weird.' I hate that. That makes my blood boil.

You can become narrow-minded. You are only open to a certain viewpoint. You put labels on people. You are moving on from one guy to the next. You might not be as open to sitting in a bar having a jar with him. It could be a personality thing too. I tend to hang around with the same type of person, although I have gone for drinks with all sorts of weirdos, and enjoyed it. Provided I can relate to what they are talking about. But that's a personality thing. I think as far as the guards are concerned, you put people into boxes. Here's a chancer or a cowboy. We have a way of slotting people in there. You might not be able to accommodate people. You just dismiss them, as someone you don't want to know. Maybe you lose out.

I always know when I'm out of my depth. Not necessarily in a violent situation, even in a verbal confrontation. Some people, I find you can't talk to.
They unnerve you. It might be the way the guy looks at you. And if you're
clearing your throat before you talk to him, straightaway you're showing
him signs that he is on top of the situation. Or, if you get off to a little bit of
a stutter. He might not have said one word to you, but the fact that you're
uncomfortable in somebody's presence ... you have to put it up to them.
You have to measure up to them.

A guy in the street might be causing a bit of trouble, he might be a hard
man. The first twelve seconds of your dealings with him make or break
whether you are going to come out of that situation on top. The way you
handle him. You have to show him you are the boss straightaway.
Sometimes I'll put my hands in my pockets and look him straight in the
eye. Come close to him. What that does, I think, is make him feel that his
aggression is inadequate. If you stand with one leg back and your fist
clenched, even though he is looking you in the eye, he is looking at your
hands. He knows exactly where he is going to hit you, if he is going to hit
you at all. If you have your hands in your pockets, he can't deal with that.
Even though he is going bananas.

You'd be terrified, but you're hiding it. I've often gone into situations
like that ... it might be ridiculous, I'll probably get the head boxed off me
some day for doing it. Maybe I'm doing something else that I'm not identi-
fying. It mightn't be that thing at all. But to analyse it, I think that's what is
happening there. You're making him feel his aggression is inadequate. He
has to re-think what he's at. That gives you an opportunity to show him that
you are in charge. Even if he lashes out. Most of these blows don't connect.
If you just dismiss them and hold on to him. Start leading him to the patrol
car as you would anyway. That can amount to an inadequacy. In other
words, no matter what you do it doesn't matter to me.

I don't always consider my own safety, but I'm always conscious about a
complaint being made against me. I'm very cautious about using force to quell
violence. It's not because I don't think that's the answer. I just don't want to be
caught on the hop. Up on an assault charge. The few years that I've had in the
job, you see fellas falling into the same trap all the time. They see a violent
situation and get a bit keyed up. You can stretch a point the odd time and give a
fella an extra little shove that he shouldn't have got. That's because the blood is

starting to boil. It's perfectly natural. But what I always do, I'm very stand-offish. I consciously step back from the situation first. I work very hard at it.

There are times when you'd see somebody coming in, maybe an old lady. She might have got a kick in the head and had her handbag taken. Talking to her you realise that she has only a couple of quid to live on for the week. You become outraged when you hear this sort of thing. Some little gurrier comes in and he's the guy that has done it. You feel like walking up and boxing him. You have to restrain yourself though, and step back.

Normally, I just walk away. Go downstairs. Don't deal with it at all. If there is violence upstairs ... unless of course the lads are in difficulty, I'd always help out if there's a problem. But if I know there's three guards and one guy up there, no matter how violent he is, I won't get involved. Because it will turn into an assault on him at some stage. It's not because I don't think he shouldn't be assaulted. I think he should be. But you can't do that. I don't think it's worth letting those people put your job on the line just for one small little episode. I don't think the public would appreciate it either. The public don't like to see people getting a clip around the ear anymore.

You often go into these flats and feel very sorry for the conditions people are living in. You see it first hand, the horrible conditions. Then, two days later, one of the young lads in the flat, that two days earlier you felt sorry for, is in the station. He has robbed a handbag. And you think he deserves everything he gets. Right up to the death sentence. You mightn't necessarily correlate one situation to the other. I don't think we consider the fact that he is doing this because of the conditions he lives in. But I think that people who suggest they are victims of their own environment are wrong. I'd say it's an issue all right, and to a certain extent it has a role to play, but a lot of decent people have come out of that environment. And they certainly get every assistance from the State. They're getting their dole, unmarried mothers' allowance ... there's a fine disposable income going into most of those houses. If they spend their day drinking it in the pub, that's their problem.

I don't know how to solve the problem. It's the great debate, isn't it? But the people talking about it on television and writing about it in the newspapers haven't a clue. They haven't seen it. They might go off on an expedition one day, have a look around and talk to these people. Talk to guards. But that's not *seeing* what happens. They're not experiencing it. They're not dealing with it. It's like isolating a laboratory sample and having a look at it. That's not looking at it and sensing what's going on.

You hear about things, programmes these people should be sent on. Just because they are only minor and petty crimes, they shouldn't be sentenced for minor crimes. That's ridiculous. The majority of crime is petty crime. It's the petty crime that's having the effect, not the major crimes. There are only a handful of people holding up banks, a handful of people killing one another. It's the petty crime that's causing the problem. And the heavy hand is the only way to deal with it. That's the way I see it. There is no answer to it, only the heavy hand. I don't mean by violence. I think stiff sentences. Take out the bail laws. Deal with them the way they should be dealt with. Make them think about what they are doing. They have nothing to fear at the moment.

At times it can be exciting. Sometimes you get a bit of a rush from it. But a lot of it is fairly routine. What was exciting to me five years ago might be routine now. The more you come across a situation, obviously the more routine it becomes. I haven't moved on in the guards enough. I don't really enjoy my day. The opposite, in fact. It's the same for a good few people of my vintage. A lot of people with the same service as myself have no interest. They're just going in and marking time. That's something that needs to be addressed. Most people, if they are left at the same thing, doing the same thing without moving forward, will definitely go stale after about five years.

I went off the boil. I had a great interest in it. I wouldn't say there was nothing like it. I knew where the pitfalls were and what was wrong with it. But I was interested. Willing to arrest fellas and go to court. Didn't really take on the system. Didn't question it that much. I got in and did what had to be done. I wouldn't be like that at all now. I still try to project a professional image no matter who I meet. But at the same time, I wouldn't go to the lengths that I went to before. I do enough just to get it done and out of the way.

The biggest problem in the guards or the reason that anybody has a problem — be it a drink problem or a personality problem — it's not the nature of the work you are doing, you couldn't get better, it's the system.

There is a problem with the system. Problems with promotion, pull, apathy, all of these. The system stinks. That's the way people look at it.

The work itself might have an effect on you, I never thought about it. Being exposed to that sort of thing all the time must have an effect. I don't know. But if I have a grievance or if I get really charged about something, it's not with this sort of stuff — the job — it's with the system. The system is breaking everybody's balls.

There is a book of rules and you follow these rules. Although, in reality, if you did, the whole thing would fall asunder. If you do something wrong, you are shown the book. You can't turn around and show them the book is wrong. Take driving the official patrol car, which is what I do. If, for example, you start work at two o'clock and somebody says, 'There's a robbery downtown.' What do you do? Run out of the station, jump into the car, start it up and piss downtown. But I don't know if there is oil in the car. I don't know anything about the car. And halfway down, if the engine seizes, the buck stops with me. The regulations say that you are to carry out a vehicle inspection before you drive the car. This is all to cover themselves. You check the spare tyre for air. You check all the tyres for air. You check all the instruments in the car. You check the handbrake, the safety belts. There are I don't know how many things to check. You can imagine me doing that outside the station at two o'clock with four shoplifters going bananas uptown, or an armed robbery going on somewhere. The system would break down. But if the car broke down they would say, 'You didn't carry out this check here.' There is no answer to it. You're wrong. You can't say this is not how things operate here. Nobody checks the car. It's a silly example. It's just one of a million regulations.

Some people think that because you're very active, you're doing everything, you're running around, you're going to court ... it doesn't necessarily mean you're a good policeman. There was an accident a few months back, a lorry ran over an old lady. Her head was squashed flat. Somebody had to go to the hospital and identify her. We had to get somebody from the family in. A good policeman would call at the neighbours house first. Make an inquiry next door. I'm not saying this is what happened. Quite the opposite. But a good guard, if he were responsible for getting a relative in to identify the remains, would call next door, find out who's there. What their circumstances are. What relation they are. Suss them out, in other words. Would they be able to handle this. Weigh up what effect this would have on them in later life.

The real active guy — out on the street, pissing around everywhere, has to get his return-of-work in, has to be the best policeman in the world — would just go up, knock on the door and say, 'Listen. Who's here? Is your father here? Yeah. Okay. Go up to the morgue. Somebody to identify. Very sorry for your trouble.' He wouldn't take stock of what is actually going on. What this guy has to witness. I'm just giving you an example of how you should hedge around a problem before getting into it. A good policeman, if he put his head together, would spend twenty minutes or half an hour driving from one side of the city to the other, going around all the relatives until he found someone he thought was fairly strong and could go up and identify, rather than putting somebody else through the misery of it. I think that would be a better day's work than bringing in forty illegal street traders uptown — with bags of oranges. And the Super upstairs thinking he was the best man in the world. You don't get credit. But if you bring in forty traders, it's all on paper. This guy is solving the problem of the traders. There's an association, they're on the Super's arsehole every day of the week about the traders, so he thinks that guy bringing them in is the ·best guard in Dublin.

Above: A garda watches the Dublin v. Derry All-Ireland Gaelic Football Semi-Final in Croke Park. Dublin have just scored.

*Left: Young girls selling cigarette
lighters in pubs. Dublin.
Above: A schools' garda in the
Muirhevnamore estate school in
Dundalk, also known as 'Little
Belfast'. The estate houses many
families fleeing the troubles in
Northern Ireland.*

Right: A sergeant and a detective pour away barrels of 'wash' — a brew made from barley and oats — at a poteen still house on the edge of a lake. Poteen, consumed by many people in rural Ireland, is illegal and the maximum fine for possession is £2,000. Connemara, Co. Galway.

Top left: Searching for poteen-makers
on the remote and deserted islands of
Connemara, Co. Galway.
Bottom left: Patrolling Lough Corrib.
Connemara, Co. Galway.
Above: An armed detective escort
for dynamite explosives work.
Connemara, Co. Galway.

Ciarán Patten

DETECTIVE. 29 YEARS SERVICE.

There's a lot of tension in the city, you're all the time expecting something to be around the next corner. You're not treated the same by the public either. You're just a handicap, an obstruction, you're in their way. They're speeding from one end of the city to the other. They want to do their own thing in their own way. You're just a burden on them. A kind of a watchdog. Annoying them.

Here, you put your hands in your pockets, walk up to a house with a cap on you and knock on the door. Even if you have a search warrant ... you'd often walk up to a door, 'How are you doing?' They'd all know you. 'Come in, have a cup of tea,' they'd say. And if you explain your case to them, they'd say, 'Go ahead. Search away.' It's completely different here. Absolutely and completely.

Time in the city means time. In the country, time just means you pass the day. People don't take much notice of time. If you have to do something at nine o'clock or half past ten, it doesn't make a lot of difference. In the city it would be an hour and a half gone. An hour and a half wasted.

The city fella might think that I have a cushy number. He'd be right. I'd agree with him on that. The city job is a different job. I wouldn't begrudge the city man anything extra he gets. I wouldn't begrudge the city fella anything.

I know fellas that came from the city and the first while they were here they were inclined to say, them and us. Us as the protectors and them outside is the enemy. I hate to hear that. I gave one fella an awful time about it. He was always going on about us and them. He tried to explain it to me. He was fully convinced that everyone outside was his enemy. If you're sent to a tough area, you're dealing with a certain crowd. And they're not nice. They're anti-police. You're inclined to treat everybody the same. You forget that ninety-something per cent of the people are genuine, law-abiding people. A few of the fellas in this job can give you an awful bad name. They don't stand back and think. We're all in it together.

If the public don't assist us, we would be useless. I've heard guards talking about the public as the enemy. I'd have to pack in the job if I thought like that.

Here, you're someone that fits into the community and has to do a little job. You might trod on somebody's toes an odd time. But after a while they'll get over it, 'He had a job to do and he had to do it.' It's accepted. You're accepted into the community. And while you're in this community they can shield and protect you. Treat you as one of themselves. Without coming too close. They're still that little bit wary. They know that you still have to do your job. You might have to deal with them in a different way. Most of them accept that. There's no problem prosecuting one of them in court. Very few of them will get sour. They know you have to do your job.

We tend not to pull up outside somebody's front door. It's a real old country thing. The neighbours are always looking out their windows. If you go to a house to make a routine inquiry and there's a woman there, she'll be worried about what the neighbours will think. Her Johnny is in trouble. Her husband is in trouble. It's a big thing. What's going to be said tomorrow. What's going to be said tonight. They get red as roses if you pull up with a summons and a neighbour's passing by. They hate it. Usually we'd park away from the house and walk back. You have to respect their wishes, as much as you can.

No matter how rushed you are, no matter how bored you are, you'll always meet somebody who will be interested in a chat. You'll always meet someone. You can chat away, you won't feel an hour going. Information broadens my knowledge of the place. If you meet a fisherman, he'll invariably want to talk about fishing. He'll start to explain one fly from another. Where he goes out on the lake. How many go out. Types of boats. Engines. The various people who go out. Where they go on picnics. All the strangers that pass through. He'll tell you all about the bad rocks, all the islands, the big noises that come by. He'll explain it all to you. If you meet a farmer, he'll go on about his cattle and sheep, this and that. And if you meet someone who has a guest house, they'll go on about tourists and fishing, and you get back to that whole thing again. There's great variety in it.

The rigid, normal police work, you can forget seventy or eighty per cent of it around here. Most of your work is nearly non-police. You're dealing with people in a different way. There's days you might have very little police work to do. You're doing more community work and social work, that kind of thing. You may get involved in doing little favours for people. Stuff that wouldn't inconvenience you, ordinary things. You might be delivering a message for somebody, an urgent message. Somebody might be in trouble somewhere and needs to get something done. You go in and you help them. You don't stick rigidly to any set pattern. You try to do as much as you can in the place.

It all boils down to the fact that you're paid to look after the place. You're paid to look after the people. I don't see anything wrong with doing favours for them, as long as you don't jeopardise your own job.

You'd have a lot of people calling to your door with little problems. They'd apologise for calling. I wouldn't mind that at all. I'd have no problems with that. Day or night, I wouldn't mind what time it was. If they had a genuine complaint and I thought I could be of any help, I wouldn't even mention it within the job. I would just go and deal with it. It could be anything. Family disputes. Somebody belonging to the family being in trouble in some other place. Something happening in another area, maybe they needed to do something in Dublin or even in England. One of the daughters, something happened to her in Galway. They would come to you at any time and talk to you about it.

You'd get a few that would come looking for you to square up something. Small little things. They were working somewhere, didn't get time to tax the car and they were caught. They were going to pay it the next day, but forgot about it. Things like that. Exceeding the speed limit. Some people are scared of breaking the law. I know people who have been driving twenty or thirty years and never had a blemish on their driving record. Something small like that, they wouldn't sleep over it. They'd take it as severe as someone else would take manslaughter. You'd know when they come to you that they'd be really distressed. I would try and find out who the policeman was. I wouldn't ask him to do anything, but I would explain it to him. I would tell him that I didn't think he'd be doing any favours for me or the job if he did anything. Nine members out of ten would let it go. Forget about it. Or treat it as a caution.

But I wouldn't do that too often. If I thought they were reckless I'd tell them straight out that they would have to take their punishment. That's your hard luck. Wait for the summons and explain it on the day of the court.

Any big thing they wouldn't bother coming to you. They would tell you about it all right. Ask you what could you do, could you help them in any way. They would nearly treat you as if you are a solicitor or lawyer. If somebody was caught for drunken driving say, he would be on to you in the morning, 'Oh Jesus. I was brought in last night, to such and such a place.' Even though he kind of understands it, you still have to go through the system with him. He'll explain it from the start — when he was stopped, breathalysed on the road, brought in by the guard and told he was arrested. He got the option in the station of blood or urine, the option of getting his own doctor. You have to go through the lot with him again.

To be drunk to a country man is to be blind drunk. Drunken driving means you would be completely incapable of doing anything for yourself. He might say, 'I only had three pints. Every other night I come in and I drink eight or nine pints, no problem. And I was brought in ...' He would probably be just over the limit. But he was still drunk. He couldn't drive. He doesn't understand that. He thinks he should be able to have twenty pints before he is drunk. He cannot understand why any law could come in and say he had three pints and therefore he cannot drive. He thinks he feels a little better and is better able to drive. Even though it was explained to him every day of the week, the laws and legislation. You can only drink so many pints.

I'd say most of them in the city know what to do. That you can only take two pints. It's very hard to put that across to the country people. I don't know, they seem to take what they are used to. Drunk is drunk and sober is sober. Black and white. There's a big difference between black and white. It's either one way or the other. They can't understand this marginal stuff.

A small little thing can upset a lot of country fellas. You have areas here where maybe no fella was caught in the last twenty years. They take it awful serious. They wouldn't sleep well at night. They'd be in to you. And they'd be wondering about it. You'd feel sorry for them. They are genuine. They're not coming and bluffing you. They are genuinely worried about it. Even up to the day in court, some of them would be sweating. They'd be in an awful state. They'd have suffered through a month or two waiting for the case to come up. In other areas they seem to be hardened to it. They say, 'Ah well. I'll be fined a few pound.' Most of the country men don't think like that. Especially in this area. Maybe you could say they are more backward than others but they aren't really. It's just their way of looking at it. Breaking the law. Maybe they break it often enough without realising it, but to be caught at it is an awful serious thing.

They seem to lead different lives altogether. Some things they take more seriously than the city people, and other things they don't. They'd be relaxed in other ways. City people tend to rush. They decide what they are going to do and then do it. And when it's over, it's over. They live by it and suffer whatever consequences. The country man is inclined to do it and then, when he has time to think about it, wonder why the hell he did it. How can he change it. He might want to change it tomorrow. I won't say he's unsure of himself but he's way more cagey. He wants to make sure that anything he does is done right.

I know this area better than I know the back garden in my home. I don't think there's any corner of it that I haven't walked and searched on a regular basis. I don't think there's one person from our area, over fifty miles, that I wouldn't know. If I see somebody that I haven't seen before, I'd be wondering, who the hell is he? He may be a member of one of the families, home from New Zealand. He might not have been home for twenty years.

Within a short time you'll find out who he is. He's a cousin. You begin to know the relations. Gel them all together. I could tell you the cousins of everybody in the place. Who's in England. Who's at home. Their names and their ages.

About two-thirds of the area is completely Irish-speaking. They'll always speak in Irish to you. They won't make an effort to speak in English. The normal conversation that they carry on, 99.9 per cent of the time, is in Irish. To change into English ... they won't relax. They won't feel as free. They automatically find a little gap between themselves and the person they're dealing with. There's a little hurdle there. Most of them have no English anyway, or very little.

In a place like this, you have the space to breathe. You can stick to a job. You never solve the crime the first day. You wait. You don't rush into it and bring in the regular suspects. You wait. Take your time. You'll find that in two or three days it'll work itself out. Somebody'll tell you something. Or you'll know something. You'll recognise it in somebody. He has the guilty look about him. You'll detect some little thing.

It's not the amount of crime that's prevented that counts, it's the amount of crime solved. That's the wrong emphasis. In an area like this, it's not because crime is not detected, it's because it's prevented. You couldn't say there is a criminal here. There might be a few youngsters who committed a crime when they were young. They were caught and stopped. There seems to be no more about it. We have very few over the age of eighteen that have committed crime. I could count them on one hand. There is no real criminal in the area. That didn't happen by accident. That was prevented. The statistics aren't there to show how it's prevented. When you look at statistics you can only see what has occurred and what was solved. There's no such thing as prevention.

You have to give everyone a chance. If somebody has done something and you dealt with him, and he didn't do it any more, you'd feel you'd really achieved something. And if he does it a second time, well, then you deal with him, and there's no more about it.

Any guard that's out the country, his first ambition is to try to get a small piece of land. To be like the natives. A bit of land, maybe get a few animals, sheep or donkeys, anything at all. It keeps the mind occupied. It's good therapy. When you go home in the evening you have to look after them. Maybe the day you're off you might spend your whole day doing it. 'Tis a good bit of exercise. Gets you away from the job. When a person is off, he should get away from the job completely. Go and do something else. Unwind and come back again when he's ready for it. He'll be a new man. He'll be way better for the job.

I came from the country all my life. Until I was eighteen years of age I never had any dealings with a guard. Never spoke to a guard. We were four or five miles away from the garda station. The guard that was there then, he was at the stage I'm at now. Winding down more than winding up. When we used to see him coming on his bike we'd run. We'd be gone. We'd be three gardens away. I don't think it was fear. Fear and respect are completely different. I don't think anybody should be running away from anybody. I don't see why anybody should run away from me. You've nothing to fear. I'd hate to think that someone was ducking me or avoiding me.

It was the same all over rural Ireland. There was the local garda, the parish priest and the teacher. They were the only strangers in any parish. The teacher was dealing with the pupils and you had to respect him. Everyone was scared of the parish priest, he was like a king or a god in the place. And the guard was the next you had to be afraid of. And you were really afraid of him. That has changed a lot. I think it's for the good.

When we find poteen, we bring it back and account for it. The superintendent has to certify that he has destroyed it. What they used to do, they'd have it all ready for the superintendent when he'd come in. There'd be a sink. But outside the lads would have a funnel going into a barrel. He'd be spilling it and they'd be gathering it again. It'd be a mortal sin destroying all that stuff.

We throw out the 'wash' all right, the brew, but not the real stuff. A lot of lads would be looking for it. That's useful for lots of things. I have a lot of requests from people looking for a drop of it. Athletes, anyone who's training, they use it an awful lot. You mix the poteen with olive oil and a small drop of iodine, to stop any infection if you have cuts. I don't drink. I never drank in my life. But I use it for muscles. I do a lot of refereeing and football. If I'm doing a serious game I put plenty of it on me before I go out. No matter how stiff you are, within ten minutes of rubbing that in, you'd run from here to Galway.

I'd hate to see it dying away altogether. All these old traditions in rural Ireland, a lot of them are dying away. There are very few now that are able to make the poteen. I hate to see a person making it wholesale and abusing it, but it's great to see traditions being carried on. Even though they may be illegal. A person making a small bit for himself, it's a tradition that was here before many of us.

There's a tendency in most places that what's illegal tastes sweeter. The pint drank after time seems to be a lot sweeter than the pint during ordinary time. And, of course, poteen's cheaper. It's less than half the price. And stronger. If you want to get drunk fairly fast, a bottle of that and you'll have no problem. It's handier to get as well. You don't have to walk far. There are areas that may not have a public house for ten miles, whereas you might have a man down the road with a 'shebeen', a little poteen place. If you have your fiver he'll give you the bottle. If you have only two pound, he'll give you half a bottle. And maybe, if you're in a bad way, he'll give you a glass for nothing. You're never going to get stuck.

You can make five hundred per cent profit on anything you make. It's a great industry for some. There aren't many doing it that way but they're the ones abusing it. We tend to clamp down on the shebeens. We hassle them until they close down. They're bad news. They're causing the most damage. Giving drink to young people. And down-and-outs. Selling it out to anyone that boozes. It causes problems, no doubt about it. I'd say it has contributed to a few deaths a year. In a small rural area that's real big business. Heavy drinking is a big burden on the community. Wives and kids being abused when they come home. To see a person suffering from over-drinking poteen, it's an awful experience. They're in an awful state. They fall into fires. It's completely different, seemingly, from the ordinary alcoholic problem.

You know a mile away the people who are going for promotion. They're ruthless. They don't care about anything. They'll do anything. They'll facilitate you, but they won't do anything in the wide earthly world that will jeopardise themselves. They won't take any risk. If our guidelines say that you hang a man at dawn, at six o'clock they'll hang him. They won't take a risk and say, 'We'll hang him at nine.' They'll hang him at six and that's it.

You have the policeman and the sergeant — they're divided into plain-clothes and uniform. Above the sergeant is the inspector, a non-commissioned officer. He's in-between. After that the whole process gets political. It's all done by the government of the day.

If there's someone that's Fine Gael, then there's no Fianna Fáil man going to promote him. Unless he's cute enough that nobody knows what politics he is. He'll play with whatever politics is in on the day. Once it gets political, it's crazy. Our job, up to the neck of the commissioner, should be completely independent of politics. It has nothing at all to do with it. No member in our job should be afraid, no matter what rank he is, to deal with a politician the same as he deals with anybody else. But you can't. There's no way. If you're looking for promotion and there's a minister wants something, by Jesus, you're going to do it. Are you not? What would you do, if you were that mad for promotion?

*Above: Preparing the evening
meal in Dromad station.
Northern Ireland border.
Overleaf: On patrol.
Connemara, Co. Galway.*

*Left: A tea-break with
explosives workers. All
explosives work must
have a garda escort.
Connemara, Co. Galway.
Above: A tea-break in the
border station of Dromad.
Gardaí have a 24-hour
armed escort from the Irish
Army in all border areas.*

Left: A detective amuses
colleagues. Oughterard,
Co. Galway.
Above: Detectives
inspect a confiscated
cross bow. Dublin.

Above: A witness is shown mug shots of suspects. Dublin.

Top right: A detective checks the sights of a confiscated replica gun. Dublin.

Bottom right: A garda waves a water pistol at his partner in a petrol station. Dundalk.

*Above: Detectives from the Drug
Squad examine confiscated
weapons. Dublin.*
*Right: A man's body is found in
a field. He apparently drowned in
a small stream, having fallen and
cracked his head on a rock.
Connemara, Co. Galway.*

Above: Confiscated
weapons. Dublin.
Right: Gardaí are called to
a 'kneecapping'. Dublin.

Des Parr

DETECTIVE. 15 YEARS SERVICE.

We had an injured party in a bookshop, a religious shop, a bible basher. A fella came in, put a syringe up to her throat and robbed the till. 'He had sad eyes.' That was all she could offer us. She didn't tell us anything else about him. He had sad fucking eyes. This guy was dying of AIDS, was sticking a syringe up to her throat, shouting and screaming at her to give him the money. And she felt sorry for him. 'He had sad eyes.' They weren't sad eyes. They were dilated pupils from being a jaysus junkie.

A junkie, he has absolutely no loyalty. Only to the substance he is abusing. And if you ever thought anything more than that of a junkie, you're an eejit. Be it in New York, be it in Toxteth — anywhere. A junkie is a junkie is a junkie. He tells a lot of lies. He's worse than a mongrel dog. He can be trained at nothing.

People are naive. They let total strangers into their offices cleaning windows. They lose £1,300 from the office. A fella with a shammy and a fucking bucket. 'I'm cleaning your windows,' £1,300 gone. 'Will you make me a cup of coffee?' He takes the money and fucks off. That's naiveté.

Old women in flats and fellas feel their boobs. They tell them they're from the Eastern Health Board. If a fella knocked on my door and said, I'm this or that, I'd want to see proof of who he is. And even when he did show his identification, I'd still follow him around. I wouldn't let a stranger walk through my house. These people walk into houses and stick their fingers up women's arses, check their tits and all this. And then rob them. They strip them down and fucking weigh them. 'Get up there on the weighing scales and I'll weigh you.' Your man and his Jeyes fluid, and a big horn on him. And then he rips them off and walks out the door. People are just naive.

You have to make humour out of it when you're dealing with some of these serious situations. Keep a certain less-than-serious attitude. If you were going to take a serious attitude in relation to every tragic event you saw, you'd be a psychiatric case yourself. Laughing at a dead body could be your only way of getting over the particular situation.

I came across a woman who jumped with her two kids into the river. A seven-year-old and a four-year-old, there in the morgue. I'll tell you, there was no humour there. It was a very, very sad day. To see a seven-year-old child in the morgue was very sad. To see a scummer that was killed in a stolen car, that's different, absolutely ... I mean, he is scum to me. They're driving through junctions at a hundred miles an hour. If they meet you with your wife and your seven kids, they'll go through you like a knife through butter. And they won't give a fuck. Not a fuck. That's honest. If I read in the paper tonight that three fellas were killed in a stolen car — great. It's three more of them gone.

The ordinary civilian would be slightly naive when it comes to things like that. Three innocent little ... you know what I mean? I'll tell you a story. I'll give you a fucking story. My sister-in-law, she was coming home from work one day with my father-in-law and there was a stolen car chase. The chase ended up with a crash, literally in front of them. Police surrounded the two fellas and kicked the fuck out of them. They got a bit of a hammering. Into the patrol car and away. I happened to be in the house that day when she came back, and I got a lecture. I got a major lecture. 'Jesus Christ Almighty. In this day and age. To see them getting the beating they got. It was absolutely disgraceful.' I fought my corner as much as I could but you couldn't talk to her.

A couple of months later, there she is, driving her father's car, a brand new Ford Escort that he treasured. Whack! Hit by a stolen car. Put all over the place. Wrecked the car. What did they do? They jumped out and ran away. It was pure honey. She has changed totally. 'Why aren't you catching these bastards? Why don't they kneecap these bastards?' He only had third-party fire-and-theft. Whatever the value of the car at the time, maybe £15,000 worth, was written off and she was nearly killed. They got out and ran away, laughed at her. She changed. She is a changed woman. She learned the hard way.

We're involved in car chases where these guys are going through red lights at eighty, ninety miles an hour. They're missing people by inches. They go through the junction, head down, and if anyone gets in the way, they're curtains. We see the destruction. And it's great to see them getting caught the odd time. Most of them will get away with it. These bastards are made of rubber. They bounce off windscreens and they jump out and run away. Like rats. It's an unbelievable phenomenon. It can't be explained. They have nine lives a week. They shatter legs. One bastard was in a wheelchair a month ago with a shattered leg. He'd crashed a stolen Opel Ascona. The leg was shattered. The fucker is going around on a bike now.

This is fact. It's happening up and down the country. I came over a bridge one night after a Honda Civic. They were flying, eighty miles an hour, maybe ninety. They tipped the kerb and the car turned over. When I say turned over, it was like a matchbox, like you just flicked it. They got out and ran away from it. You could not tell the make of the car it was so damaged. There wasn't a straight panel on it. And they ran away from it.

The authorities are a different ball game. There are guys that were never on the street in their lives. They know nothing in relation to street work. They were never out there. They went from office to office, rank to rank. And they're sending down circulars, 'This is the position. If this situation arises on the street, this is what you're to do.' And they know nothing. Our own superintendent. Very nice fella. Love the guy. I'd marry him in the morning. But he was never on the street in his life. He's done nothing. He's a lovely fella, but he has never walked the street. If he came on a situation in the morning, he wouldn't know how to handle it. The public wouldn't understand that. They would think, okay, you're a superintendent, you must have been very efficient, a great policeman all your life.

There is a sense of camaraderie. Even fellas you wouldn't like, you would go to their assistance. If you're involved in a situation, you might have a bit of a row or whatever, but there's no fella going to get up on a box and say, 'I think you were a bit excessive in relation to this or that.' That doesn't happen. If you were involved in a situation and there was a complaint and an investigation into it, no fella would hang you out to dry. No fella would turn around and say, 'I saw you throwing a stone at a stolen car.'

If you catch someone doing a robbery, you catch a hold of him and give him a good fucking slap. Show authority. You'll have no problem with him. Take control of the situation and the chances are you won't get touched. If you show him you don't know what you're at, he's saying to himself, 'If I can hit this fella one slap in the mouth I'm away, I've escaped three years in prison.'

Any guard that's assaulted is a fella that's laid back. Maybe he's a recruit or he's kind of naive-looking. That's the man that'll get assaulted. I was assaulted once. I had three years service at the time. I battered your man later. But he gave me a good couple of clips. I've never been assaulted since.

We went into McDonalds one time and there was a bloke on the counter. He had a brush and he was battering the staff. We went up and battered him. If we went in and said, 'Get down off that counter, please. We're the guards. Get down,' we'd have been wide open. If you don't show authority you're bollixed. It's a minor part of the whole job. It's not an everyday occurrence. But when it's needed the police are good at it.

If you're a criminal and you're breaking into cars, you're doing snatches or you're robbing banks, it doesn't pay to fight with the police. You complicate the whole situation. You're better meeting the police on the street, 'How's it going? How are things?' This type of crack. Let's say I happen to have a warrant for you. And we get on great. We have a working relationship. I'd say to you, 'Leo, I have a warrant. You'd want to get yourself organised 'cos you're going to be picked up, you're going to be locked up on it.' But if you're a bollix and I know there's a warrant for you — bang! You're lifted there and then. Night court. Custody. If you're into crime on a full-time basis it doesn't pay you to fight with the police. We were in a certain hotel on Paddy's Day and there were certain fellas buying us drink — criminals, street traders, all these wankers. Why fight with them?

You have to have contacts. You have to be able to talk with these people. If there's a serious crime, you have to be able to say, 'Look, what was the position here?' In police work there is no line down the middle. It's not black and white. You're dealing with individuals. You're dealing with human situations. It was never made to be black and white. If you're dealing with a particular set of rules in relation to say, chess, golf or rugby, they're black and white. When you're dealing with human situations, they're not.

It's a game really. A person who does burglaries, say in offices, how are we supposed to have a personal grievance against them? It's not affecting me directly. There's no violence committed against anyone. That doesn't take anything out of me. Whereas handbag snatchers, for example, I would have a personal grievance against. They're generally hated. A handbag snatcher would be hated by the average criminal. Robbing bags off women. It could be your mother, my mother. Your sister, my sister. It's a despicable crime.

I might have a grievance against Johnny so-and-so. If I come across Johnny so-and-so in a situation, lovely. But once I get into my car to go home, Johnny so-and-so does not come near my thoughts. Once I'm finished I have nothing to do with it. There are some and the job is their life. I have my life. My family. I enjoy shooting. I enjoy fishing. I play a lot of golf. I love drink. I love Gaelic football. The World Cup. I'm into a bit of photography. I have all that. I go in, do my eight hours and I forget it. Some fellas would do a few extra hours, for *nothing*. Sit around the office. Come in days they're not working. I wouldn't do that. I have a wife who would say to me, 'What are you at? What's your problem?'

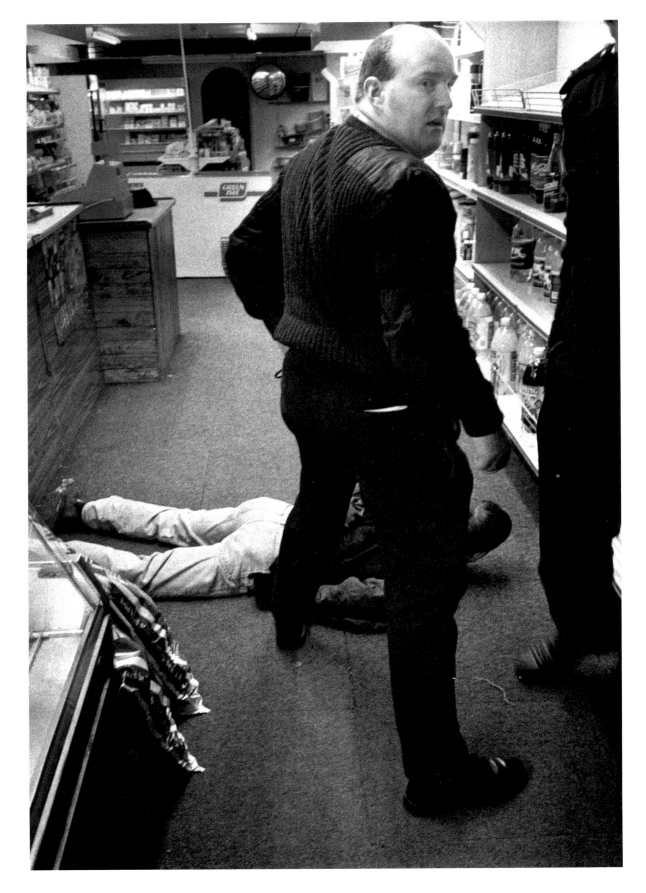

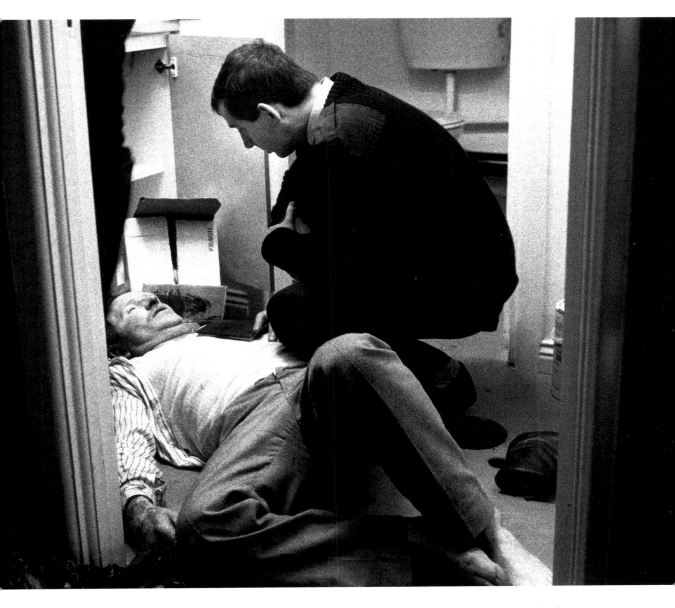

Left: A youth is arrested after a struggle. He was attacking and attempting to rob a shopkeeper when a passer-by alerted gardaí. Dublin. Above: An ambulance crew prepare to bring the injured shopkeeper to hospital.

*Above: A victim of a Stanley
knife attack is brought to
hospital. Dundalk.
Right: A mugging victim
makes a statement. Galway.*

Left: After a 'few' drinks,
a man jumps into an empty
Royal Canal. Dublin.
Above: A victim of a hit-
and-run accident. Dublin

Left: Gardaí prepare to enter hostile territory. Dublin.
Above: Glue-sniffing. Dublin.

Top left: A girl makes an assault complaint against a neighbour. Dundalk.

Bottom left: A man talks to a community garda about his neighbours, who are selling drugs. Dundalk.

Above: A schools' garda calls to remind a woman of her forthcoming court appearance. He is taking her to court over her son's non-attendance at school. Dundalk.

Overleaf: Thieves climb drainpipes at night and break into shops from the rooftops. Dublin.

Ken Mulhall

UNIFORMED GARDA. 11 YEARS SERVICE.

We got a report of a chase going on in the suburbs. The radio was going mad. Cars coming from everywhere in pursuit of this armed robbery. We were told to head towards the city, it was possibly going that way. We were just coming up to the bridge and, straight in front of us, the robbers' car came out. Straight in front of us. With about twenty cars coming after it. We came out, sharp right, sharp left. We pulled into the third slot, and off we went.

There was sirens, there was lights, there was noise, and there was panic. And the next thing, control gave out a message. I learned later the message was, 'Uniform men drop back. Shots fired.' At this time my driver was overtaking number three car and we were behind SDU [Special Detective Unit]. There was the raiders' car, SDU, and then us. In all the panic, with the adrenaline pumping, I said to my partner, 'What did he say?' He said, 'I don't know. Don't mind him.' Flying along.

The next thing, the SDU car in front swerves over to the wrong side of the road. I said, 'Where the fuck's he going?' I looked up and there was a gun pointing back from the passenger seat, firing at us. I literally pushed my partner, thinking I'd pushed the car across the road. He says, 'What the fuck are you at?' 'There! ... Look! ... Shooting at us!' 'Oh fuck.'

We kept up behind them. And there was a lot of shots fired back at the pursuing guards. The adrenaline was there and you just never thought of it. It was just go! Go! Go! Go!

Another SDU car met them coming in the opposite direction and there were shots exchanged. The raiders' car hit a parked car, did 180 degrees, and came straight back towards us. But we were all right because the SDU were in front of us. Until the SDU pulled over to the other side of the road and we were left with this Mazda 626 burying towards us. Straight up the nosepipe we went. Whack! Pal's car goes up our left wing. Goes up and comes down to rest. Which left me, as close as you are to me, with a fella called Johnson pointing a gun in my direction.

My partner had bolted out the door. I couldn't get out my door. I couldn't get across the two seats so I bolted for the back seats with the top half of my body face down on the back seats. I put my two hands over my head. What I imagined my two hands over the back of my head would do to stop a bullet, I don't know. I really don't know. The shots went cling, clang, clang. I could hear it from outside and I could hear it over the radio. It was frightening. So I just lay there. It seemed to be eternal but I'm sure it was only a minute or so. I was lying there and everything stopped except the shouting on the radio.

I looked up and there's a fella in a white shirt and a red tie and a gun in his hand saying, 'Are you all right?' I crawled across the two seats, out the driver's door and collapsed on the road. There was a posse of cars behind us. All the guards were running forward to have a look. I was lying with the back of my head against the back door, 'What the fuck happened there?' I was in a state of shock. And some guard started shouting, 'Get a fucking ambulance up here. This man's shot.' I went, 'I'm not shot. Am I?' I honestly didn't know if I was or not.

I looked round at my back at the amount of blood and what turned out to be brain matter and hair belonging to Johnson, who was shot in the head from twenty yards away. When he pointed the gun at me an SDU man shot him straightaway. One bullet. Back of the head. His head exploded all over my shoulder.

We all arrived up in casualty. The x-rays and all the tests were done. Four of us were sitting there thinking, 'What a rush. That was something.' Which hopefully we'll never see again in our career, but at the time it was very exciting. You were physically shaking. Physically and emotionally shaking. Traumatised.

Everybody was all right, thank God, bar the two gougers that were killed. We were put into a back room and were sitting there going, 'Fuck. That was crazy.' I actually went in and looked at one of the dead bodies and said, 'You fucking bastard. May you roast in hell.'

The room was like a grey haze, you could cut the smoke in it. The sister arrived in with this woman in her mid-thirties with a big white coat. 'This is Dr Kelly from the psychiatric wing.' From then on we knew that, yes, there is something here. She sat down, she talked bullshit to us. We thought it was bullshit 'cos the police would never admit that type of thing could ever affect you. It does have an effect. It does affect you, in a big way.

For two or three weeks after it I was waking up about five times a night thinking I heard somebody in the back garden. I thought I was losing my brain. Then I met up with several people who were involved in shooting incidents and they all had exactly the same experiences. Very deep shock, very severe trauma. And you won't get over it no matter how macho you are or how much you joke about it. It does leave a significant mark for the rest of your life. I can still see exactly what happened that day. If I was a video recorder you'd see it yourself.

Top left: Sheriff Street housing
estate where many stolen cars
end up. Dublin.
Bottom left: A detective retrieves
a stolen car from Sheriff Street
estate seconds before it ends up in
flames. Dublin.
Above: Two patrol cars are
grounded after being stoned. Dublin.

*Left: A detective goes on an early
morning drugs raid, armed with
'The Fireman's Key' — the key to
open all doors. Dublin.*
*Above: Gardaí from the Drug
Squad watch the flat of a heroin
dealer from a nearby disused
building. Dublin.*

Jim Flynn

DETECTIVE SERGEANT. 28 YEARS SERVICE.

I think like a policeman all the time. You don't have any other way of thinking. If you take any couple of young people and you put them to work in a particular section ... there's a controlling influence in that section. A domineering influence which can give a line of thinking they didn't have before, give them answers to questions they didn't have before. You're conditioning them and the conditioning itself will cause them to change.

The thinking will change. And if the thinking changes so will how they express themselves, how they answer questions and not answer questions. React to a situation or not react to it. It changes their whole perspective. If you're at that long enough you obviously have a different way of thinking.

Protection has to be one of the main concerns. Protection of ourselves. Anything we do is subject to scrutiny so we have to be careful. We can't have a policeman wrecking cars at night-time because he's had a few drinks. We can't have him going down to the local pub, shouting and screaming and creating a row. I wouldn't expect any of my people to do that. If they did, there's something lacking. And if there's something lacking, they shouldn't be there. They certainly shouldn't be with me.

We're employed by the State to protect people within the State, so we must protect them as best we can. And to do that, we must know the limitations as to where we can go and where we cannot go. We couldn't very well have somebody who was going to be a danger to themselves or to us. Some fella with suspect thinking or suspect ideas. Can't have it.

There is a bond there. Probably due to a degree of dependency on each other. You give somebody something to do, you're depending on them to do it. Likewise, if you tell someone to do something, they're depending on the fact that what you're telling them to do is all right, and it's going to work. It's not the same way as a fella might do it in an office with a lot of paperwork. Or a fella building a house. It's a different thing. There's a lot more depending on it. There's an element of danger in this all of the time.

We don't have the same rigid attitude to police work as others. Uniforms dictate a certain type of appearance, they dictate a certain type of behaviour. You look well and you represent whatever you represent. We're trying to do the opposite.

Common sense and do what you're told, that's what you need on this unit. You have to be non-aggressive but capable of aggression. People will react to you the way they find you. Going in to search a house, if you have an aggressive attitude towards them, they'll react aggressively. You'll have problems. You'll have trouble. You'll have rows. You'll have bad relationships with them. Go into a house and do what you're supposed to do. Leave out the aggression. Aggression stems from fear. People sense it. There can be an element of fear in a lot of these places, there's no contradicting that. You can be fearful going in. Not afraid, fearful. You never know what you might find. You always have to be aware of needles and syringes. Little men can have fierce weapons. He doesn't need to be a big man to create big problems. But once you get in, you should be able to control it. Take it as it is and use no more force than is necessary. Minimise the aggression in even getting into a place. Do it in such a way that you do it quickly, do it well and leave it at that, in preference to hassling people in an aggressive way.

We can be very aggressive. You hear people abusing fellas, giving out, calling them all kinds of shits and muckas. Serves no purpose. But on the other side of the coin, if you do get into a house or a place where you're going to have a lot of hassle, you'll have problems, or problems will arise. You're quite capable of dealing with them as aggressively as you need to. You do whatever is necessary to survive.

Usually the crowd I'm with will do what I do. If they don't see me doing it, they won't do it. If the fella gets smart, abusive, and you have to take him, you take him. You use whatever force is necessary. Only on rare occasions would you ever leave him behind. You can't afford to back down, unless in the interest of survival. It's expected of us. If we go somewhere, we go and do whatever we're going to do. If we don't continue to do that, if we're ever seen to lose one, or two, or three. We're on a loser. They'll all take us on then.

Threats come in two categories. Those that count and those that don't. I think you only threaten someone that you feel may be unjust to you. Usually the fear is that you're either going to be attacked or there may be some danger there that you might not fully appreciate. It depends on what the problem is. If it's a fella who is aggressive, and he's likely to use a hammer, or a hatchet, once you have him under control that resolves the problem. Healthy fear is a very good thing. Otherwise you can be foolish. You could walk into issues that you shouldn't walk into. You need to be careful in relation to where you go or how you do it. It's not unknown that they would try to set us up.

We also have a great advantage in that we know the people we're dealing with. We know them all and they know us. We know their strengths and they know ours, with very few exceptions. Protection is in knowing. Some fella said one time, 'It's not a man's physique you have to watch, it's his mind.' That's where the danger lies.

I believe that you must treat all people with respect until such time that they decide they won't treat you with any. As long as you behave rationally and reasonably towards them, you'll always minimise the problems. They know us. They know if we go into a place we're not going to find anything that wasn't in it. We're not going to say they said anything they didn't say. They know we're going to play it straight with them. If they're caught, they're caught and if they're not caught, they're not caught. That's the beginning and end of it.

They don't have this fear of falling for something they mightn't be responsible for. And over a period of years where you've been consistently doing what you're supposed to be doing, people accept that whatever you're going to do, you're going to do it straight. And if you come, the reason for coming is justified. If you search, it's justified. They're not going to get into any difficulties over anything they haven't got. You can't afford any kind of a suggestion that you either did or said anything that you shouldn't have done or said. Because the thing spreads very quickly. A fella will go to jail and he'll tell a story. In jail everybody has it. You might survive one story. You might even survive two. But you won't survive indefinitely. Life is a lot easier, in a rough place like this, if you play it straight. You don't have to watch your back. There's no fella coming after you because of something you did that you shouldn't have done.

If they think you're going to do something you shouldn't do, it automatically puts up barriers. They have to watch you. They have to be careful. They can't afford to have any kind of a reasonable attitude towards you. You're a threat. You're like an old dog, an old bad dog that might bite them. So they have to keep their distance. Keep the dog at bay. Treat them reasonably well. If they treat you that way, you'll survive most issues.

The whole scene is violence. Violence and fear. It's dominated by fear. You can sense it. I think we learn to accept seeing violence. There was a young lad the other morning, five or six years old, in the flat, the mother spaced out in the bed, her head back, a needle stuck in her arm and bleeding. Abscesses on her legs. The other fella lying on the couch, spaced out. And the little fella sweeping the floor in the middle of the flat. That is far more violent than a fella lying below, dead in the street. There's a greater degree of violence in that. It's a living violence. The other is an act. In a short space of time something happened and ... boom!

I'm as capable of violence as anybody else. More so maybe, if it's necessary. You'll always have the odd one who'll stand out and put it up to you. How far is he going to go? He might do it next time. I think you need to let them know you're willing to do it if it becomes necessary.

One fella had a bit of a habit of producing needles. He was told that he was in danger of death. It might be necessary to shoot him if he produced any more of those dirty needles and threatened police with them. I told him, if I thought there was a likelihood that he was going to reach anyone with a dirty needle, I'd shoot him. He stopped. If you have to contend with working in that environment all of the time, you have to have a set way of thinking. You wouldn't tolerate people to the same extent, talking crap. If you have something to say, then say it.

Policemen tend, over the years, to talk police business. They drink together and they talk together. They socialise and talk police. You'll never be finished talking about what so-and-so did. So-and-so went to jail. The criminals are the same. They spend an awful lot of time talking about the police, in the prisons. We do lose, I'm sure, some of the finer aspects of socialising. It's a consequence of living this way. If you were working in a different area, a suburban station where the people are nice, you'd have a different attitude to life.

If you have spent years talking to people about certain matters which a lot of them don't want to talk about. Drugs. Were you selling drugs? Did you break into that house? Did you hit that fella with a hammer? This kind of thing stays with you. You just can't walk away and leave it behind. It's still there. You apply the same way of thinking outside working hours as you do in working hours, I've no doubt you do. As to how it might have affected me, I'm quite sure it has. It has conditioned me to think a certain way. I don't know how the fella next door might think or how he might resolve some bit of a problem he might have at home. I'm inclined to resolve it as I'd resolve an issue in town. I'm very reasonable in town.

Another element that's essential for successful police communications is trust. Our business is based on trust. When people decide to tell us we ensure it's never divulged. The trust takes years to build. You have it and practise it in the police. You have it and practise it at home.

They trust you with something that may be a danger to themselves. A fella might say, 'I'm involved with such and such a body, with such and such an amount of stuff.' Or, 'If I tell you something will you promise not to do anything? Don't touch him because he's a friend of mine, but you can have *him* because he's not. Will you agree to that?' And, over a period of years, you have not been found to be wanting. With the result that they come back to you again. They trust you. People talk for different reasons. Some talk because they need to. Some talk because they want to. Some talk out of fear. Some talk out of a kind of insurance for themselves, for the future. More to get their own back on somebody. Some fella ran off with his wife. Some wife ran off with the husband, whatever. If they don't trust you, they don't tell you anything. If you breach the trust it gets around, word spreads.

If they could establish who the informers were in the different areas, they'd burn them out. They'd half beat them to death. The practice of trust and confidentiality is paramount to the survival of a successful police unit. If you practise that at work, you ought to be able to practise it at home.

The reaction that young people or children are most fearful of is somebody exploding. A policeman can sit and listen. Go in and talk to a fella who's after abusing children. You can sit and listen to him telling you how he did it, why he did it and you don't explode. How much more difficult is it to listen to a child who's after breaking a window?

There were times when some people would have had an interest in doing away with me. I'd be a reasonable target. When you get over a couple of those hurdles, and you survive them mentally — you're not shaking afterwards, you're not looking for an office job, you're not looking to be taken in off the street — when you get over those, an awful lot of little things don't matter.

There'd be fear that it might happen. Then fear that you mightn't be able to do something about it. And then anger. To the extent that you would try to counteract it. Protection. What kind of protection? On one occasion somebody had a bit of an interest in me. I used to take the dog walking, late at night, and I got to carrying a gun. Sometimes I would and sometimes I wouldn't. The way I figured it afterwards ... guns create dependencies. Some people will find that when they have a gun with them, they'll feel superior, more secure. Maybe they don't see the dependency but there is one. Carrying this old gun in my pocket, walking the dog at night, I'd be thinking if somebody did want to do anything, how would they do it? But after a short time, I didn't bother carrying the gun any more. I figured the futility of it. I realised how easy it would be, if somebody did want to do it. A gun wouldn't stop them. They'd take you anyway.

There was one last year, one the year before. Both taken seriously. And quite a bit at stake for those involved. What I would emphasise is that of any of the incidents that occurred, none were personal. They were all based on where I'm working and what I'm working at. Police business. A couple were in danger of going to jail for long periods.

One of them has since gone and one of them's on the way. Both had an idea that if I wasn't around, that was the way out of their problem. They made some endeavour to find someone who would do that for them. It's an awful lot of money. It was necessary to counteract them.

Having got through the initial stages, and looking at it now, if the attempt had been made it might have been viewed differently. If somebody had attempted and missed, I would have had other considerations. I might have had to get out of the police. Or I might have had to do something that I wouldn't want to do — take up an office job, something like that. The attempt wasn't made. I told somebody that would have had a contact in that circle, that I knew something was in mind and that it shouldn't happen. I think that stopped it.

I've always worked in crime. I've been down there with the criminals for years. They know me. I knew their grandfathers. No doubt a lot of them would have a degree of respect for me. Maybe doing bits of turns now and again. If they wanted something done, they could come and ask me. If I wasn't going to do it, I'd tell them. But at least they could come and ask. Somebody dies and they want somebody out of prison. Maybe we could do something.

I go to some of the funerals of the people who died from the drugs problem. Some of those are very moving ceremonies. You don't know till you've gone and seen a junkie dying or being buried, a young one, maybe with kids, and seen the families, the church, the surroundings. But there's a borderline. You could be intruding too. If we didn't feel we were welcome by the families of the people who died, we wouldn't be there. But I think it adds an air of respect to an otherwise, maybe, black kind of a situation, where nobody's going to say much good about them.

They are all God's children. If the time is right for them to get caught, or the time is right for them to die, God will design that. God's timing is perfect. If we do what we should do and do it straight, the rest is up to God. It's not up to us.

*Left: A cigarette-break on
the docks. Dublin.
Above: The public office in
Store Street station. Dublin.
Overleaf: The night shift.
Oughterard, Co. Galway.*

Above: A sergeant cuts turf for the oncoming winter. Connemara, Co. Galway.